D0877377

Lessons from the Bard

To Anna —
To thine own self
be true!

Best —
Marie

Lessons from the Bard

What Shakespeare Can Teach Us about School District Leadership

Marie Wiles

ROWMAN & LITTLEFIELD
Lanham • Boulder • New York • London

Published by Rowman & Littlefield
An imprint of The Rowman & Littlefield Publishing Group, Inc.
4501 Forbes Boulevard, Suite 200, Lanham, Maryland 20706
www.rowman.com

86-90 Paul Street, London EC2A 4NE

Copyright © 2024 by Marie Wiles

All rights reserved. No part of this book may be reproduced in any form or by any electronic or mechanical means, including information storage and retrieval systems, without written permission from the publisher, except by a reviewer who may quote passages in a review.

British Library Cataloguing in Publication Information Available

Library of Congress Cataloging-in-Publication Data

Names: Wiles, Marie, 1963– author.
Title: Lessons from the Bard : what Shakespeare can teach us about school district leadership / Marie Wiles.
Description: Lanham : Rowman & Littlefield, [2024] I Includes bibliographical references. I Summary: "This book makes connections between the five Shakespeare plays most frequently taught in US high schools and the essential elements of being an effective educational leader"—Provided by publisher.
Identifiers: LCCN 2023039024 (print) I LCCN 2023039025 (ebook) I ISBN 9781475869996 (cloth) I ISBN 9781475870008 (paperback) I ISBN 9781475870015 (epub)
Subjects: LCSH: Educational leadership. I Shakespeare, William, 1564–1616—Criticism and interpretation. I Leadership in literature. I Shakespeare, William, 1564–1616—Influence.
Classification: LCC LB2806 .W55 2024 (print) I LCC LB2806 (ebook) I DDC 371.2/011—dc23/eng/20230920
LC record available at https://lccn.loc.gov/2023039024
LC ebook record available at https://lccn.loc.gov/2023039025

♾ ™ The paper used in this publication meets the minimum requirements of American National Standard for Information Sciences—Permanence of Paper for Printed Library Materials, ANSI/NISO Z39.48-1992.

Contents

Foreword

Paul Grondahl

What does an upstate New York suburban school district superintendent know about William Shakespeare? And, more specifically, how could an examination of five of Shakespeare's best-known plays help inform, illuminate, and offer guidance for the challenges facing today's school leaders in these tumultuous times?

Methinks Dr. Marie Wiles doth protest too much, to paraphrase that playwright from five centuries ago. I admit, I was skeptical.

Alas, brevity is the soul of wit, to borrow another great line from Shakespeare. I'll get right to the point. *Lessons from the Bard: What Shakespeare Can Teach Us about School District Leadership* is an unexpected gem. It surprised me, held my attention, and made me think in new and fresh ways about what it means to strive to be an effective school leader. Dr. Wiles writes in an accessible style with clear-eyed prose. She knows exactly what she wants to say, and she says it well—and economically, too. Her book does not try to be something it is not. She concedes at the outset that she is not a Shakespearean scholar. She is not attempting to contribute to the vast pool of data-driven research into educational techniques or strategic methodologies. She offers a caveat that even Shakespeare-averse educators who may harbor a phobia about the plays from high school days need not fear the Bard in her iteration. Nor is this a how-to manual. It presents itself in more of a whisper than a shout, while its message strikes a chord. Dr. Wiles writes with a welcome sense of humility.

Dr. Wiles, who taught Shakespeare as a high school English teacher three decades ago, has been an educational leader for twenty-seven years and a superintendent for more than two decades. She understands that the job of being an effective school leader is as much art as science. Her book is meant to explore "a more personal side of leadership," she writes in the preface. It delves into "the power of relationships, the magic of effective communication, the dangers of giving into our 'tragic flaws,' and the beauty of truly loving the work that school leaders do on behalf of the children and communities they serve."

Wiles draws instructive, real-world lessons from five of Shakespeare's most popular and frequently taught plays: *Romeo and Juliet*, *Macbeth*, *The Merchant of Venice*, *Julius Caesar*, and *Hamlet*. In addition to offering a reader-friendly summary of each play, Wiles zeroes in on scenes, themes, and characters that offer food for thought for school leaders. For example, she details how all the adults in *Romeo and Juliet* fail the young, star-crossed lovers because their thinking is rigid and out of touch with the reality of youth. This failure leads to tragic results. "Perhaps we need to devote fewer resources to trying to change how adolescents think and focus on creating learning opportunities that explicitly develop their self-regulation skills." Flexibility, understanding, keeping an open mind, and treating each young person as an individual with unique needs is key. *Romeo and Juliet* is a cautionary tale about what happens when this does not occur. As Wiles writes, adults devolving into political polarization and culture wars—exacerbated during bitter feuds over vaccination mandates during the coronavirus pandemic—represent a sure path to anger, failure, and recrimination. "This willingness to pay attention to what young people are saying requires a certain amount of humility and humanity, key characteristics of any good leader."

I thought I knew quite a bit about William Shakespeare. I studied his plays extensively as an English major during my bachelor's degree and master's degree programs and wrote numerous essays about the plays' universal themes. I worked on the stage crew one summer during college at the acclaimed Oregon Shakespearean Festival in Ashland, Oregon, and have seen a dozen of the Bard's dramas performed on stages from Seattle to New York City. We have brought Shakespearean scholars to the New York State Writers Institute at the University at Albany, where I serve as the Opalka Endowed Director. As a journalist and author, I dip into the Shakespeare canon to illustrate a point or for inspiration. Nobody in the English language delves into the human condition in a more profound and entertaining way than Shakespeare.

After reading *Lessons from the Bard*, I came to view both Shakespeare and the work of school leaders in a new light. Dr. Wiles has provided a novel perspective on the Bard that will fill the heads of school leaders with beautiful language, challenging scenarios, and practical ideas. Permit me to conclude: To read or not to read, that is the question. Read it. You'll be saying bravo, anon.

Paul Grondahl is the Opalka Endowed Director of the New York State Writers Institute at the University at Albany, a columnist at the Albany Times Union, *and the author of several books.*

Preface

The idea for this book is based on a talk that I gave at the March 2022 conference of the New York State Council of School Superintendents. The council asked me whether I would present one of three "ignite" sessions as part of the keynote program on the first morning of the gathering. As the name implies, an ignite session is supposed to spark some interesting thinking on a timely topic in a fast-paced ten-minute talk. My superintendent colleagues and I were still leading our schools through the insanity of the COVID-19 pandemic, so my assigned topic was high on everyone's list of priorities for students, staff, and ourselves: social-emotional wellness. At the time, I had been an educational leader for twenty-seven years, twenty-one of those as a superintendent, and I was not (and still am not) an expert in social-emotional wellness, so I decided to draw on my background as an English teacher to help me get started, which led me to Shakespeare.

Truthfully, I am not really an expert on Shakespeare either. When I took the stage at the conference, it had been close to thirty years since I led a group of students through the journey of one of Shakespeare's masterpieces. But I brushed up on his work and drew on three plays (*Macbeth*, *The Merchant of Venice*, and *Hamlet*) to illustrate points about social-emotional wellness for superintendents. My preparation for the talk made it clear to me that I was just scratching the surface of what we could learn about leadership from Shakespeare's works.

The purpose of this book is to dig a little deeper into what Shakespeare can teach us about being good school leaders. I decided to explore five of his plays, the same five that are most frequently taught in high school classrooms in the United States. There is a certain amount of poetic justice here. We ask our students to wrestle with these texts to learn about complex characters and profound literary themes captured in the lovely poetry and prose of Elizabethan English. Why can't school leaders dig into those same texts to see what wisdom might be unearthed? In this book, I remind readers of the timeless stories of *Romeo and Juliet*, *Macbeth*, *The Merchant of Venice*, *Julius Caesar*, and *Hamlet* as windows into various aspects of being an effective leader.

To be fair to my readers, who are likely to be school leaders or those aspiring to be, I want to be clear about what this book is *not* about. It is not about a strategic plan for being an effective leader, and it is not a "how-to" guide for winning and keeping that desired leadership position. This book does not contain any charts and graphs or even much data to suggest how best to lead a school or district through a change process. There are plenty of exceptional educational scholars who have published volumes of robust research about these and other leadership topics. This book explores a more personal side of leadership. It takes into account the human condition, the power of relationships, the magic of effective communication, the dangers of giving into our "tragic flaws," and the beauty of truly loving the work that school leaders do on behalf of the children and communities they serve.

Finally, I just want to address any residual fear that readers might have from their own high school experiences of reading Shakespeare. I know that these fears exist based on the initial response from many colleagues at the conference where I spoke. Those fears went something like this: "Shakespeare: that's too lofty for me," or "I hated Shakespeare in school," or "I never did actually read those assigned plays." This book does not require anyone to be a Shakespeare scholar. It simply asks readers to become reacquainted with some timeless stories, memorable characters, and remarkable feats that can be viewed as parallels to the remarkable feats that school leaders perform each and every day.

Acknowledgments

Like the plot twists of so many Shakespeare plays, the origin of this book is pure happenstance. Before sitting down to write *Lessons from the Bard*, I had never seriously considered writing a book, much less one that attempts the unlikely link between Shakespeare's classics and modern school district leadership. But the deed is done and there are many to thank.

I will begin with the colleague at the New York State Council of School Superintendents who suggested that I might be someone capable of presenting an energizing and informative ten-minute talk (a.k.a an ignite session) as part of the opening of that organization's winter conference in March 2022. Close to two years elapsed before I learned it was my long-time fellow superintendent and friend Chuck Dedrick, the executive director at NYSCOSS, who threw out my name to the conference planning committee. I am grateful for his confidence in me and for the endorsement of that committee, led by Phyllis Harrington, who was president of NYSCOSS and conference chair at the time. I also want to thank Theresa W. Moore, an associate director at NYSCOSS and the individual who turns conference planners' ideas into reality. She was the one who reached out to ask me to present and the first person to whom I floated my offbeat idea about basing my talk on Shakespeare. That "ignite" talk turned out to be the spark for this book.

I also want to thank Jay Goldman, the editor of *School Administrator* magazine, published by the American Association of School Administrators. It was Jay who saw the title of my talk in the conference program (*To thine own self be true: What Shakespeare can teach us about our own social emotional wellness*) and asked me to write a six-hundred-word essay that would appear in the June 2022 issue of that magazine. It was that brief article that prompted Tom Koerner at Rowman & Littlefield to contact me and say, "I'd like to help you turn this idea into a book." A few encouraging conversations with him helped me overcome my skepticism that writing about school leadership and Shakespeare was something that I could actually do and that such a book would be one that anyone would want to read. His enthusiasm for the idea and remarkable willingness to believe in me, someone he barely knew, compelled me to get the work done. I hit "submit" on the completed manuscript exactly one day shy of a full year from his thumbs-up on my proposal. This book would not have come to be without Chuck, Theresa, Jay, and Tom.

I believe that those who choose to make their living in schools are remarkable for their kindness, compassion, support, and capacity to inspire. That has overwhelmingly been my experience during the fifty-five-plus years I have been connected to school, as either a student or an educator. So, I want to thank some of my stand-out teachers who inspired in me a love of literature and an appreciation of good writing and critical thinking (and the ability to do them). Among them are Patricia Dawes, one of my elementary school teachers at St. Mary's in Clinton, New York. She was the first to see promise in me as a reader and writer. Many years later, I had the privilege of calling her a colleague when I became the superintendent of the Clinton Central School District and she was the director of curriculum. Elizabeth Lemieux (whom everyone called Wiz) was my AP English teacher at Notre Dame High School in Utica, New York, and demanded clear thinking and even clearer writing. Even though I was often completely intimidated by her obvious brilliance, she stands out as an educator who made me a better thinker and writer. While there are many other fine educators who had a positive impact on me when I was an undergraduate English major at Temple University, a graduate student for secondary English education at SUNY Albany, and a doctoral student in teaching and curriculum at Syracuse University, I would not be an educator today without Pat Dawes and Wiz.

I also wish to acknowledge the five hundred or so students whom I had the privilege of teaching in the early days of my career as an English teacher in the New York Mills Union Free School District. They, too, were an inspiration for this book. Although they were my students in the late 1980s and early 1990s, I still vividly recall our shared journey through Shakespeare's *Romeo and Juliet, Macbeth, The Merchant of Venice*, and *Hamlet*. These were journeys that started on a bumpy road of resistance with complaints like "This language is impossible to understand"; "I have no idea what is going on"; and "Why do we have to read this?" But by the time we read, watched, discussed, and debated each play, I would often hear, "Wow, this is an amazing story!" and "This is the best thing we've read all year!" I still recall and revel in the moments when the timeless stories and stunning poetry and prose of Shakespeare's work "kicked in" for students and their eyes lit up with understanding and appreciation. I channeled those moments many times while writing this book.

I also wish to acknowledge some of my closest colleagues in the Guilderland Central School District, who knew I was spending many early mornings before the start of the school day and most weekends working on this project. My amazing assistant, Deb Sim, and her colleague, Linda Livingston, provided sympathetic ears when I lamented my sometimes slow or halted progress on this project when the realities of my role as superintendent of schools filled all of my time and cognitive space. I also want to thank members of the district office team, who were also supportive, but who dished it out in the ego-checking form of good-natured ribbing about the "loftiness" of my topic. Among them are Neil Sanders, now retired assistant superintendent for business; Regan Johnson, assistant superintendent for human resources; and Rachel Anderson, assistant superintendent for curriculum and instruction. I also wish to acknowledge the members of the Guilderland Board of Education, who knew I was laboring on this writing project during much of my "free" time. I value their support and encouragement.

Being a superintendent of schools in the Capital Region of New York State has its blessings; chief among them is being a part of a tight-knit group of professionals who understand the power of collaboration and teamwork. I appreciate the comradery of my twenty-three fellow superintendents in this region and their kind support of me as a colleague and as a contributor to the field through this book and otherwise. I particularly wish to thank now-retired BOCES district superintendent Anita Murphy for her unwavering support and no-nonsense pep talks whenever a hint of self-doubt threatened to derail my work. I am also grateful to Mr. Paul Grondahl, the director of the New York State Writers Institute, who is an award-winning author and neighbor, who agreed to write the foreword to *Lessons from the Bard*. He is generous with his time and talent in the writing community, and I am honored that he is the person who launches this project.

Finally, it seems rather inadequate to simply acknowledge and thank my family. There really are no words to capture how much they mean to me in our busy, everyday lives, and how much they contributed to the completion of this project, beginning with their acceptance of my need to dip into our already scarce family time to write. Beyond that, my husband Tim and teenage son, Ben, served as patient sounding boards for my ideas, insightful commentators on my analytical assertions, and expert editors of my prose. Tim, a librarian by trade, is an accomplished author in his own right, having published numerous articles and two books in his beloved field of baseball research. He has also helped countless baseball researchers with their writing projects: assisting with research, fact-checking, and offering feedback on early drafts. He is an outstanding editor and helped me immensely by reading and commenting on my first draft of this book.

My most cherished moments in writing this book were when Ben, then a sophomore in Guilderland High School, would gingerly knock on the guest room door where I set up my makeshift writer's workshop, to see how the work was going. He would sit on the bed and ask to hear the latest paragraph or two and offer excellent suggestions to make the text clearer or more interesting. While he claims he does not like to write, Ben has a way with language that makes his English teacher/ superintendent mother and librarian father proud. So while I never intended to sit down and write this book, it was a rare opportunity to bring together sometimes disparate areas of my life: student, English teacher, superintendent, wife, and mother. One lesson that I learned while writing this book is how important it is to be willing to open the door when opportunity knocks. For me, it resulted in a feat of happy happenstance, bringing my loved ones into my work in unexpectedly fulfilling and joyful ways. I am so glad I opened that door.

Introduction

Shakespeare lived close to five hundred hundred years ago, but his work remains remarkably relevant to twenty-first-century life, particularly for those who lead schools in the United States. How can this be? Other than a fleeting reference to a few characters either going off to or returning from the university, William Shakespeare does not write about schools or education. He himself likely attended only a grammar school until about the age of fourteen, and it is doubtful that during that time he would have gained much insight into what the school's headmaster did. And it is certain that he would not know anything at all about what a school principal or a superintendent even is, let alone what these individuals do in the day-to-day routine. So what leadership lessons can Shakespeare offer to school leaders nearly half a millennium after he lived? It turns out, plenty.

The purpose of this book is to explore the school and district leadership lessons that can be gleaned from five of Shakespeare's most well-known and frequently taught plays: *Romeo and Juliet*, *Macbeth*, *The Merchant of Venice*, *Julius Caesar*, and *Hamlet*. Why is such an endeavor worthwhile? Many who write about current events draw on Shakespeare's stories and characters to draw parallels to leaders in business, industry, and politics. You can find references to Macbeth's ambition, Hamlet's indecision, Shylock's greed, and Caesar's lust for power in recent publications just by performing a simple Google search. The proliferation of references to Shakespeare's work is a testament to the timelessness of the stories he tells, the characters he captures, and the brilliance of his poetry and prose. But no one has tried to tie Shakespeare's work to the work of those whose job it is to lead schools.

In the pages that follow, this book will tread into some new territory by making a connection between the five plays most frequently taught in schools in the United States and the essential elements of being an effective leader of schools. The idea is that school leaders might be able to learn a few things from the very plays they require their students to read, study, and discuss. And while the role of school or district leader may have some similarities to those who rise to the top in business or politics, there are some fundamental differences for school leaders. Their mission is not to make money or to amass power but to shepherd community resources to teach children. This altruistic mission justifies a special look at what it takes to be a quality school or district leader and what Shakespeare's works might have to say about it.

In addition to being frequently taught in schools, these five plays are featured because they are familiar and accessible. All of the titles have been remade or adapted into modern productions, whether on stage or in feature-length movies. The most familiar example is *West Side Story*, both a stage musical and a movie based on the story of *Romeo and Juliet*. These plays, their characters, and many of their most famous lines are frequently referenced and quoted in articles, opinion pieces, song lyrics, and even vintage television sitcoms. Any *Gilligan's Island* fan will recall the ship-wrecked crew's rousing musical reenactment of Hamlet's central problem and existential question, "to be or not to be?" So no one reading this book needs to become a Shakespeare scholar, or even to reread these plays, in order to appreciate the school leadership wisdom that can be gleaned from them. The text provides helpful short narratives as a starting point.

The five plays selected for this book explore themes that are profoundly relevant to those who are or who aspire to be school leaders. Those themes include everything from understanding how the adolescent brain works to managing money and resources to leading with a clear sense of purpose. Each chapter of this book focuses on one of the five plays and the leadership themes that can inform the work done by principals, superintendents, and other school leaders. A brief synopsis of those themes, by play, follows.

SUMMARY OF FEATURED PLAYS

Chapter 1 considers the tragedy of *Romeo and Juliet*. The backdrop of the play is a centuries-old feud between two families, the

Montagues and the Capulets. Members of these households, including the people who work for them, despise the other family with a venom that regularly poisons the streets of Verona with barbed comments, bloody brawls, and murder. Shakespeare never tells us why these families hate one another so, but that hatred defines their entire worldview—to the detriment of all. It is in the stew of this divisiveness that the impetuous adolescents, Romeo and Juliet, meet and fall in love. Their love is instant and intense and also doomed to fail because of their own immaturity and the failure of the adults to guide and support them.

As such, their story holds many lessons, almost all of them cautionary, to those whose job it is to educate children. The tragic deaths of the young people, set in the context of a highly polarized community, hits close to home today. Serving young people is at the heart of what school and district leaders do; lately, however, that service is carried out in a polarized climate that might be just as irrational as the feud between the Montagues and Capulets.

Some of the important lessons to be considered in chapter 1 include understanding the adolescent brain, setting appropriate expectations for young learners, committing to truly listen to what young people have to say, and understanding what it means to support student growth and development without inspiring outright rebellion or enabling their overdependence on help. The adults in the play utterly failed their children; no school leader wants to own such failure.

Macbeth is the subject of chapter 2. It is another play ending with many deaths, but one that feels profoundly different from *Romeo and Juliet* in tone and tenor. There is little love, laughter, or lightheartedness in *Macbeth*, the story of a man and woman who are consumed by unbridled ambition inspired by a prophecy of three witches that Macbeth will be king of Scotland. Spurred to action by his power-hungry wife, Lady Macbeth, the title character murders the sitting monarch King Duncan and takes the throne for himself. In very short order, Macbeth is wracked with guilt and paranoia. He is forced to commit more and more murders to protect himself, and he is tormented by the apparition of the ghost of his one-time best friend Banquo, whom he had murdered. Macbeth becomes a tyrannical leader isolated from all his former friends and associates. A bloodbath devolves into a civil war, sending Macbeth and his wife spiraling into madness and death. If ever there is a story illustrating what not to do as a leader, *Macbeth* is it.

One of the leadership lessons to be drawn from this tale is the intersection of ambition and school leadership, including some special considerations of what it means to aspire to a leadership role for women. Another lesson is the importance of maintaining one's social and emotional wellness and the role that positive relationships and supportive networks play in doing so. The tragedy of *Macbeth* also provides some memorable reminders about the necessity to get enough sleep. The Macbeths' actions during the daylight hours render them unable to sleep soundly at night, and their inability to rest at night renders them incapable of functioning rationally during the day. The Macbeths show us that exhaustion is the enemy of effectiveness. The same can be true for those who lead schools.

In chapter 3, *The Merchant of Venice* is the next play to be considered for its school leadership lessons. It is the only comedy to be included in this analysis. As a comedy, it is filled with humor, romantic love, some clever role reversals (complete with cross-dressing characters), and a mostly happy ending. However, the play also has a darker side. The central action of the play is rooted in an ancient and enduring hatred for someone who is "other." In this case, that person is Shylock, a Jewish moneylender who seeks revenge against a wealthy Venetian merchant, Antonio, who has failed to repay his debt to him on time. It may seem that a play that explores themes of hatred, greed, revenge, and the exclusion of those who are different is an unlikely platform for any discussion of school leadership, but the opposite is actually true.

The Merchant of Venice illuminates many leadership lessons, from the technical to the philosophical. For example, there is something to be learned about managing money and financial stewardship, as well as knowing and following the rules, laws, and regulations that dictate the proper ways to get things done. The play also is a vehicle for self-reflection because it can inspire individuals to look inside themselves and ask what kind of leader and person they are. Do they welcome and affirm each and every person, even those who are "different"? Do they keep their word? Are they capable of mercy? These are all needed skills and essential questions for school and district leaders.

The fourth play is *Julius Caesar*, a classic and timeless tale about political power. It is the subject of chapter 4. This relatively short play, in which the title character lives only until Act III, contains all of the trappings of a misguided lust for power and popularity. As the supreme leader of the Roman Empire in 44 BC, Caesar is cursed with an enormous ego, excessive pride, and the need to be adored by his minions.

These character flaws inspire acts of conspiracy and insurrection among those who dislike him and fear that he will become a cold-hearted tyrant. Julius Caesar's untimely death is the result of his inability to listen to good advice from trusted allies because he is so caught up in his need for recognition and approbation.

Not only does the powerful Caesar fall prey to false flattery in the play, his longtime and trusted friend Brutus is corrupted by fake news. The conspirators in the play convince Brutus that Caesar is dangerous by sending him forged letters with made-up tales of his corruption. To continue the theme of how language can manipulate the thoughts and actions of others, Mark Antony, Caesar's one loyal friend, whips the common people of Rome into a frenzied mob who vow to avenge his death in the famous speech beginning "Friends, Romans, countrymen, lend me your ears." A bloody civil war ensues.

There are many lessons for school leaders in *Julius Caesar* that fall into the realm of political awareness and communication skills. School leaders need to be open-minded and willing listeners, thoughtful and truthful speakers, and excellent judges of character so they can discern fact from fiction and truth from falsehood from the many stakeholders who will want to share their thoughts and influence action. School and district leaders also need humility and the wisdom to recognize their own fallibility. Caesar was convinced that he was all knowing and all powerful, and it cost him his life. Such hubris among school and district leaders can in fact cost them their livelihood. An analysis and discussion of this play provides insight into how such pitfalls can be avoided.

In chapter 5, the final play to be considered is perhaps Shakespeare's greatest masterpiece. It is *Hamlet*, a tragic tale of a Danish prince who is called on to avenge his father's murder. The murderer is his own uncle, Claudius, who did the traitorous deed to become king and to marry Hamlet's mother, the queen. Ironically, the action of the play is the story of inaction. Until the very end, Hamlet is unable to follow through on the very clear purpose that he has been given by the ghost of his father. He spends most of the play trying to confirm the guilt of his murderous uncle and incestuous mother. And even when that guilt is confirmed, he does not act on his purpose, which causes him so much mental distress that he contemplates his own suicide in the famous "to be or not to be" soliloquy.

This play provides a useful window into the challenges of being a school and district leader on one level because educational leaders, like

Hamlet, tend to be fundamentally good people. Unlike Macbeth, Caesar, Shylock, and Tybalt, for example, who have deeply flawed characters that lead to death, destruction, and misery for themselves and others, Hamlet is a young man who is a good and faithful son who loves his country, family, and friends without ego or ambition. The best school leaders are the same, and so the important lessons from *Hamlet* are about avoiding the mistakes that Hamlet made. Those lessons are about leading with purpose, delivering on promises, making sound decisions, being true to oneself, and living a life that is beyond reproach.

STRUCTURE OF EACH CHAPTER

Each chapter of this book begins with a brief explanation of why the particular play is a useful springboard for discussing school and district leadership. That explanation is followed by a synopsis of the play focusing on the characters, elements of action, and Shakespeare's use of language that highlight the relevant leadership lessons for educators. So the summaries of the plays are illustrative to make the points about school leadership, rather than an exhaustive recounting of the tale. The rest of each chapter is broken down into the specific leadership lessons found in each play along with the current, practical, real-life implications of those lessons. Each chapter includes a summarized list of those leadership lessons and ends with a list of discussion questions that can provide the starting point for discussion among current school and district leaders and those aspiring to be (or not!).

So many of the lessons to be learned from these five plays by Shakespeare can be characterized as "cautionary"—examples of what school leaders should not do to avoid the disasters that are the hallmark of tragedy in drama. But avoiding trouble is not the goal of the very best school and district leaders. The real goal is to serve a school community honorably and effectively by working from a place of genuine commitment to the overall well-being of each and every child. While that work can be daunting and all consuming, it is also work that brings profound joy and satisfaction. In the pages that follow, these selected Shakespeare stories will illuminate the highs and lows of school and district leadership and ideally inspire an opportunity for thoughtful reflection for those who are or aspire to be leaders in schools and districts.

Chapter 1

Romeo and Juliet

My only love sprung from my only hate.
Too early seen unknown, and known too late!
Portentous birth of love it is to me
That I must love a loathed enemy.

—Juliet, Act I, Scene 5

Who doesn't know the story of *Romeo and Juliet*? It is perhaps the most famous love story of all time and certainly one of the most frequently read of Shakespeare's plays in America's high schools. Students are regularly asked to read or watch the play and think about what it can teach them about literary themes like love or fate. But can the play teach school leaders anything about their work? The answer is a resounding yes. The first of many reasons for this is that *Romeo and Juliet* is about young people, and serving young people is at the heart of educational leadership.

This chapter will explore some key elements of the play, including the developmental characteristics of adolescents, the role of adults in setting realistic expectations for them, and the devastating impact of divisiveness and polarization. We will also consider what it means to guide, support, and listen to young people—or, more accurately, what it means when that guidance, support, and listening fails or is absent. *Romeo and Juliet* is a tragedy. By the end of Act V, essentially all of the young characters are dead by senseless murder or ill-fated suicide, so the lessons for school leaders are cautionary ones.

SUMMARY OF *ROMEO AND JULIET*

The play opens with a fight in the public square of Verona. It is the latest in a string of brawls instigated by members of two families' houses, the Capulets and Montagues, who have been feuding for generations for reasons that are never revealed. The prince of Verona is angry and frustrated by the constant disruptions to the city's peace and declares that going forward anyone who fights in Verona's streets will be put to death.

That same evening, Romeo, a Montague, shows up uninvited to a party hosted by the Capulets in hopes of seeing Rosaline, a young woman whom he loves but who is ignoring him. Instead, Romeo sees Juliet, is overcome by her beauty, and quickly forgets all about Rosaline. Romeo and Juliet meet and instantly fall in love.

After the party, neither Romeo nor Juliet is able to sleep. Romeo is wandering the streets of Verona and decides to scale the wall of the Capulets' property and sees Juliet on her balcony. What follows is perhaps the most famous love scene in all of literature; it culminates in their plan to secretly marry the very next afternoon with the help of two trusted adults, Juliet's nurse and Friar Laurence.

Everything goes downhill from there. Shortly after Romeo and Juliet are married, Romeo and his two friends, Mercutio and Benvolio, encounter Tybalt, Juliet's hotheaded cousin, who is angry that the trio had attended the Capulet party the night before. Inevitably, their argument turns to fighting, and Tybalt kills Mercutio. Romeo, who initially did not want any part of the violence, is enraged that his friend was murdered; he ends up dueling with Tybalt and kills him.

Earlier in the play, another young man, Paris, made his appearance at the Capulets. Paris is from a wealthy family and seeks permission from Lord Capulet to marry Juliet. The father is thrilled, but Juliet's mother less so because Juliet is only fourteen years old. Ultimately they agree it is a great opportunity for her and for them to have their daughter marry so well. When her mother shares this news following Tybalt's death, the already-wed Juliet is distraught and defiant, and she initially refuses; her father is furious with her and is ready to disown her.

When the prince learns that Romeo has murdered Tybalt, he banishes Romeo to Mantua, rather than killing him as he previously decreed. Juliet's nurse tells her that Romeo killed Tybalt and that he will be banished. Juliet is awash in emotion, trying to reconcile the revelation that her new husband has killed her cousin; however, her love for Romeo overshadows his guilty act. That evening, before Romeo leaves for Mantua, he and Juliet consummate their marriage; Juliet is heartbroken and desperate that he must go away to avoid his own demise.

Her desperation leads her to Friar Laurence, who has a risky plan to help the two lovers reunite. Juliet is to drink a potion that will put her into forty-two-hour-long sleep so deep that she will appear to be dead. While asleep, Friar Laurence will send word to Romeo to come back and get Juliet so that they can go together to Mantua.

With this plan in place, Juliet tells her family that she will marry Paris after all, and the Capulets hastily plan the wedding. Bravely, Juliet drinks the potion. On the morning of her wedding day, she appears dead; great sadness fills the Capulet home, as wedding plans become funeral plans. Juliet is laid in the Capulet vault to await Romeo's return. However, Friar Laurence's message to Romeo detailing the plan is never delivered. Instead, Romeo is visited by a family member who tells him of Juliet's death.

Distraught, Romeo purchases some poison and returns to Verona with the plan to lie with Juliet forever. When he arrives at the vault, Paris is there. He has flowers that he wished to place with the young lady who was to be his bride. Paris attempts to capture Romeo, who he knows should not be in Verona. The two fight, and Romeo kills Paris. He then enters the tomb, sees his beloved Juliet, and, thinking her dead, drinks the poison he brought with him and dies. Moments later, Juliet awakens and sees her dead lover. Friar Laurence, who rushed to the tomb to try to salvage the plan, is unable to convince Juliet to leave the tomb, and he runs away. In order to be with Romeo forever, Juliet takes his dagger and kills herself.

By the end of the play, Mercutio, Tybalt, Paris, Romeo, and Juliet are all dead. Only then, when all of these young lives are lost, do the two families vow to end the feud and live together in peace.

ADULTS FAILING CHILDREN

One of the most shocking elements of *Romeo and Juliet* is the almost complete failure of every single adult character to appropriately meet the needs of the young star-crossed lovers. Whether the adults were too harsh in their demands for obedience or too quick to succumb to the ever-changing whims of the young people, all of them made decisions and took actions that doomed Romeo and Juliet and most of their friends.

First there is Lord Capulet, who is determined that his very young daughter marry Paris, a man she has never even met. To be fair, arranged marriages were common in the 1500s—wealthy families used this practice to secure the financial stability of the next generation—but the father's anger and his rush to disown his daughter when she objects are shocking. In his wife's presence, he says to Juliet:

Hang thee young strumpet, wretch!
I tell thee what: get thee to Church on Thursday
Or never think to look me in the face.
Speak not, reply not, do not answer me
My fist trembles. Wife, we thought us blessed
That God had lent us this single child,
But now I see this one is one too much,
And we have a curse in having her
Disgusting harlot.

Lord Capulet says this to a daughter who has never once disobeyed him or his wife. As soon as she did not agree with his plan for her, a plan that in his mind was the right one for all concerned, he set the stage for her to take drastic measures to avoid it.

Lady Capulet was only marginally better in supporting Juliet. She initially objected to having Juliet marry Paris given that she was barely fourteen but quickly came around to approve of the idea as soon as Paris pointed out that there were other fourteen-year-olds in Verona who were already mothers.

Even adults who were arguably on the side of Romeo and Juliet ultimately failed them. Juliet confided in and trusted her nurse. It was the nurse who helped orchestrate the secret marriage between Romeo and Juliet when she saw how love-struck Juliet was, but then, when Romeo is banished, she quickly changes her mind and seeks to persuade Juliet to marry Paris instead. The three adults in Juliet's life all stop listening to her, disregarding her needs and pushing her to take matters into her own hands, with some help from Friar Laurence.

As a member of the clergy, Friar Laurence should have known better, but he is at the center of aiding and abetting the hasty and impetuous plans of the young lovers. He barely stops to question Romeo's complete turnabout in his love life. In less than twenty-four hours, Romeo's obsession for Rosaline, one so strong he risked attending a party held by his family's archenemy to see her, turns to Juliet the moment he sees her. Friar Laurence knows this, but rather than counseling the young couple to stop and think through their plan, as one would expect from the clergy, he not only agrees to marry them but actually does so. All of this in one day!

Friar Laurence is also the adult who provides Juliet with the drugs to make her appear dead so she can avoid the arranged marriage to Paris. Ironically, the risky part of the plan works perfectly, but the seemingly straightforward part—getting word to Romeo in Mantua—fails miserably because Friar Laurence either did not know about or didn't account for the travel restrictions in and around Mantua because of plague.

At the end of the play, Friar Laurence races to the Capulet tomb, ostensibly to be with Juliet when she awakens, but instead he sees the horrific scene inside. There lie the bodies of three young men: Tybalt and Paris, both killed by Romeo, and Romeo himself, who took his own life with poison. When Juliet awakens and sees her dead husband, Friar cannot convince Juliet that she should leave the tomb and her lost love. His opportunity for encouraging rational thought is now gone. But even at the end, he does not seem to take responsibility for his role in all of this death, blaming it on "a greater power . . . that hath thwarted our intents." At this critical moment Juliet tells him to go away, and, in a final act of failure, he leaves her to take her own life.

GREAT EXPECTATIONS

So what lessons can school leaders learn from the actions and reactions of the adults in *Romeo and Juliet*? One important lesson might be about our expectations for our students. Just as Lord Capulet had his mind set on what the "successful" future for Juliet would be (marrying a wealthy noble), school leaders (and parents too) can have a fixed idea of what student success looks like: excellent academic grades and extensive participation in extracurricular activities and athletics, all leading to acceptance at a quality college, where it all begins again.

Even though there is ample evidence that a pathway like this one is not the only way that students can find success in career and life, it is often the only message that they hear in school. In addition, conforming (or failing to conform) to that traditional set of expectations for success in school has many unintended consequences for students' social and emotional well-being. The highest-achieving students often report being "stressed out" due to the pressure of getting good grades and competing with other high-achieving students with the hopes of ranking higher than their peers. Students often report staying up all hours into the night to complete homework, study for tests, or complete presentations. All of this work takes a toll on the students' well-being.

The experience of students who either cannot or will not buy into the traditional definitions of success or wish to pursue a different pathway can also threaten their social and emotional well-being. In the most extreme cases, these could be students who openly rebel against the norms of school and find themselves saddled with discipline referrals, detentions, or suspensions from school. Think about how Lord Capulet was so quick to want to banish Juliet from their home and life because she didn't wish to comply with his vision for her future. Can it be that schools sometimes do that very thing to students whose vision of their future doesn't match the authorities' vision? Juliet took extreme measures to avoid her father's chosen path for her; sometimes students who feel betrayed, ignored, or alienated in school make similarly perilous decisions that can affect their physical, mental, and emotional health.

There are also myriad students who are neither high-flying achievers nor outright rebels. They may get decent (but not great) grades. They follow the rules and stay "under the radar." Perhaps their interests fall outside the traditional offerings at school; they play a sport for which there is no school team, or they play a musical instrument that is not part of the school program. Perhaps they are from a culture with different values and expectations for success in school and life. For many of these students, they are in school but may not feel that they are part of the school. They may feel invisible; if so, that is a failure of the adults in school.

On the other end of the continuum is the kind of failure that happens when adults, with all the very best intentions, do too much for students in school. Ironically, helping too much can have terrible consequences. In the play, the nurse and Friar Laurence are the prototypes of this kind of failure. Clearly both of these characters cared deeply about Romeo and Juliet. Their care was returned with affection, trust, and respect. These adults knew the youngsters well and were ready to do whatever necessary to help them achieve their goal to be together as husband and wife.

Both nurse and Friar Laurence took great risks with their superiors (the Capulets and the church) and with the authorities in Verona. Arranging a secret wedding, orchestrating the consummation of the marriage on the very day the husband (Romeo) killed a Capulet family member (Tybalt), and procuring potions to feign death to avoid Lord Capulet's wishes are all dramatic and courageous actions to help the two young people. They each took on great risk and went far above and beyond their defined responsibilities. But rather than rushing to find solutions to Romeo and Juliet's problems, as trusted adults, they might have been in the best position to convince the young lovers to slow down, think through their situation, and try to talk with their parents to help them understand. In their race to do too much for Romeo and Juliet, they unwittingly aided in their untimely demise.

There are adults in school, often in supporting roles, who are also devoted to the students they serve. Those students are often ones for whom learning does not come easy or who need additional help to manage their behaviors. Students often become very attached to the teaching assistants, aides, nurses, and others who can provide extra support for them. The support that students need and get can make all of the difference in their success in school, so long as they are not simply doing the work for those students and unintentionally teaching learned dependence. The consequences of learned dependence are certainly not as dramatic as the outcome of this play, but it effectively lowers expectations for what students can achieve on their own later in life. When students of any ability level don't increase their capacity to become more independent, it does limit their opportunities as adults.

UNDERSTANDING ADOLESCENTS

Another important lesson that school leaders can take from *Romeo and Juliet* is the importance of understanding youth development, particularly that of adolescents. Research has taught us a great deal about the adolescent brain, which by the age of about ten is physically almost fully grown but far from fully developed. In fact, as Dr. Laurence Steinberg, one of the leading experts on adolescent development, has said regarding brain development, "Adolescence is the new zero to three."[1] By that, he asserts that the well-known period of brain malleability and development attributed to the earliest years of life is followed by an equally malleable period of development during the ages of approximately ten to twenty-five. Further, research suggests that just like the zero- to three-year-old brain that is affected by the quality of the experiences of the child, so, too, is the adolescent brain sensitive to its experiences, for better or for worse.

According to Steinberg:

> [T]he adolescent brain undergoes particularly extensive maturation in regions that regulate the experience of pleasure, the ways in which we view and think about other people and our ability to exercise self-control. These three brain systems: the reward system, the relationship system, and the regulatory system are the chief places where the brain changes during adolescence.[2]

This is a time of great opportunity and vulnerability for our youth depending on the quality of their experiences. Shakespeare wrote *Romeo and Juliet* without the benefit of having read psychological research on the adolescent brain, but he seems to have captured the essence of that period perfectly.

Romeo and Juliet were clearly driven by their desire for reward: being together as husband and wife. Their quest is both an emotional and a sexual reward; their willingness to take dramatic risks is breathtaking. Romeo and his friends crash the party of their enemies, the Capulets, with the hope of seeing his beloved Rosaline, only for Romeo to fall in love with Juliet instead. Later that night he risks all possible consequences and climbs the wall of the Capulet home to speak with Juliet on her balcony. After being banished from Verona, he risks entering Juliet's home and room on the night of their wedding. Three times in the play, he impetuously and violently ends lives—first Tybalt's, then Paris', and finally his own. Never once does he pause to think about the long-term implications of his actions. Imagine if he waited just a few minutes in the Capulet tomb; Juliet would have awakened, and they could have lived happily ever after in Mantua.

Juliet captures the essence of the adolescent. She defies her parents for the first time ever when they speak of her marriage to Paris. Her parents are shocked and angered by her uncharacteristic refusal. She further shows her adolescent spirit when she lies to her parents, telling them that she is going to see Friar Laurence to seek the sacrament of confession (for her defiant behavior) when she is really going to see the friar for assistance in rejoining Romeo. She engages in the risky business of drinking the friar's potion that will again deceive her parents into thinking she is dead so that she doesn't have to marry Paris. She, too, is unable to pause and think through the consequences of her actions. In the end, she cannot have her "reward," Romeo, so, like him, she takes her own life.

The actions of the characters are extreme, woven together brilliantly by Shakespeare for dramatic effect, but certainly parents and educators alike have seen adolescents take foolish risks with the hope of rewards: the approbation of peers or the affection of a first love interest. Parents and educators have seen young people with inexplicable mood swings, outbursts of defiance, engaging in risky behaviors in which they experiment with smoking, vaping, drinking, drugs, excessive speed when driving, texting while driving, and so on. Yet adolescence is also a time when we see young people filled with energy, enthusiasm, creativity, and joy. As Steinberg puts it, adolescence is "like driving a car with a sensitive gas pedal and bad breaks."[3]

Herein lies an important takeaway for school leaders: Since adolescence is a time of tremendous brain malleability, it means that schools (and parents too) can have an enormous impact on students' development during this time. They can provide experiences that capitalize on their susceptibility to productive growth while creating environments that protect adolescents from themselves. All of this is likely even more important today, when many young people are battling to recover from the effects of the COVID-19 pandemic, which shut down schools and interrupted lives in ways not seen since the early 1900s.

One approach that has gained traction across the United States during the early post-pandemic years is the explicit teaching of social-emotional wellness. Schools have adopted programs like the Positivity Project,[4] which offers lessons each week on one of twenty-four character traits meant to enhance students' capacity to get along with their peers, engage meaningfully in their academic learning, and develop skills like perseverance and perspective. The Collaborative for Social and Emotional Learning[5] is another resource for school leaders to get ideas and guidance about effectively promoting the social and emotional growth of students.

Another approach is to consider reorienting schools to focus on the aspect of the adolescent development that is still evolving during high school years: self-regulation. Research has shown that self-regulation and the traits that it influences (like determination) are some of the strongest predictors of success. As Steinberg has pointed out, "People who score high on measures of self-regulation complete more years of school, earn more money, have higher status jobs, and are more likely to stay happily married."[6] Yet schools generally do not do a very good job of explicitly teaching this skill.

While there are some promising practices to promote the development of self-regulation, they are far from standard fare in most American high school classrooms. According to Steinberg, there are exercises designed to improve aspects of executive functioning, practices to increase "mindfulness," and strategies to boost self-control and the ability to delay gratification. Aerobic exercises and exercise that involves a strong mental component, like yoga and tae kwon do, are also promising avenues for developing better self-regulation. Students who participate in these kinds of activities tend to do so outside of school with private providers, so access is limited to those who have the financial means to do so. Interscholastic sports can also be an effective way to develop self-regulation skills, but they often are limited to those with interest and skill in the menu of sports available in any given district—in other words, only a subset of our students. Also, playing sports involves buying into a culture that may have negative elements and even more unhealthy cultures of achievement and conformity.

Physical education classes are a potential venue for strengthening the self-regulatory skills of students. Since every child is required to take PE, making the development of self-regulation explicit in that curriculum holds promise. One conclusion that research has confirmed is that simply telling students about the dangers of engaging in risky behaviors like taking drugs, using alcohol, and having unprotected sex (like we do in typical health classes) is not an effective way of preventing students from doing these very things. They know the risks but take them anyway because their need to seek "rewards" is so much stronger than their self-control.

As school leaders, knowing what makes our adolescents tick and how they think (or fail to) can and should help us make better decisions about how we allocate our resources, what we include and emphasize in our curriculums, and the advice we give to parents when we seek their partnership in supporting their children's success. Perhaps we need to devote fewer resources to trying to change how adolescents think and focus on creating learning opportunities that explicitly develop their self-regulation skills. After all, schools have students during the exact time in their lives when that portion of their brain development is most malleable and most likely to have a positive effect. Ignoring this reality is a missed opportunity.

What might have been the outcome in *Romeo and Juliet* if the Capulets had spent less effort on planning parties and weddings designed to dictate Juliet's future? What if they chose to listen more closely to their daughter's wishes and took the time to help her think through the consequences of her immediate love for Romeo? Perhaps doing so would mean that fewer of those party plans would have consequences that tragically turned into funeral plans. Also, this parental script is harmful to some students who are different, such as LGBTQ students, whose hopes and dreams might be quite different from their parents' expectations.

There are so many "if only" moments in Romeo and Juliet, but even better reasoning and a little more delayed gratification might not have made a difference. As Juliet points out, important truths are "known too late." Too much of the drama of the play is dictated by the ancient feud between the Capulets and Montagues. No one is taking time to be thoughtful, rational, or patient. Ultimately, the actions and reactions of too many of the characters are clouded by hate. This fact brings into focus the dangers of divisiveness and polarization.

DIVISIVENESS AND POLARIZATION

The final lesson that school leaders can take from the tragedy of *Romeo and Juliet* is about the devastation that divisiveness and polarization of adults can wreak on young people's lives. The entire play is premised on a feud so old that no one in the play seems to know the reason for it; Shakespeare gives us no clue about why the families despise one another so profoundly. And even though he shows the audience glimpses of hope that at least some of the characters are tired of the conflict, the full realization of how destructive the feud really is does not come until it is too late.

The prince of Verona is certainly tired of the constant fighting that comes with the families' "rusty hate." That is why he decrees that whoever is caught fighting again will be killed. The Ladies Montague and Capulet also try to hold their husbands back from getting involved in the fray at the start of the play. After the prince makes his decree, even Lord Capulet lets on that he is tired of what Montague calls the "ancient quarrel" when he admits to Paris "'tis not hard I think for men so old as we to keep the peace."

But the hatred has so permeated the houses of the two families that these hints suggesting the feud is no longer relevant do not make a difference. After all, it is the servants of the families who begin the first quarrel in the play, and it is Juliet's beloved nurse who breaks the news to her that Romeo is "the only son of your great enemy." It is Juliet's cousin Tybalt who seeks revenge against Romeo for attending the Capulet feast, even after Lord Capulet attempts to convince him to stand down. Too many of the supporting characters in the play have accepted that the feud will define their worldview, and they act accordingly. So when Romeo and Juliet demonstrate that their instant and overwhelming love can overcome hate, no one appreciates that truth until they (and several other young characters) pay the ultimate price with their lives.

Over five hundred years later, the world is still filled with people taking sides. The bitter politics of the late 2010s and early 2020s can be seen and heard daily in the news. At the global, national, regional, and local levels, all the way to the schoolhouse door, too many adults have entrenched themselves in positions that are far left or far right and are unwilling or unable to listen to those who might see the world differently from themselves. Too many adults then have their positions reaffirmed and validated by following publications, cable news channels, and social media outlets that echo what they already believe, regardless of what evidence (or the lack of evidence) shows.

Of course, not everyone is engulfed in extreme polarization, nor was everyone in the city of Verona actively taking sides with either the Montagues or the Capulets. But when enough of a community is engaged in battle, it can and does affect the whole community, including the schools and the students within them.

Perhaps the best example of divisiveness that affected public schools occurred as school leaders were reopening them as the COVID-19 pandemic gripped the nation and the world. While there were certainly many who were relieved and appreciative when educators found ways to safely reopen schools after the March 2020 shutdown, many others ferociously argued against the very safety protocols that made opening possible: social distancing, universal masking, regular testing, and vaccinations. The most polarizing of these measures were masking and vaccinations.

The pandemic was a time of fear, uncertainty, and isolation. During the period when essentially all schools in the United States were closed, educators made nothing short of Herculean efforts to offer a continuity of instruction for students as they hunkered down at home. Learning transitioned to fully remote education with varying degrees of effectiveness. Parents (especially women) left the workforce in order to stay home with their young children. Parents and guardians who could work from home struggled to balance their own responsibilities with assisting their children in their learning. People all over the world were getting sick and dying. It was a dreadful time.

Schools that were lucky enough to reopen in September 2020 did so under strict guidelines for social distancing, mask wearing, and limitations on all sorts of activities like athletics, music, and even eating lunch in the cafeteria. Many students continued to learn remotely or learned through a hybrid model in which they alternated learning from home and coming to school. While many families were relieved that schools were back in session at some level, there were also many who were convinced that the pandemic was not real and that the health precautions were, at best, unnecessary and, at worst, actually detrimental to students' mental health and social development. A simmering discontent among factions who supported and didn't support the health and safety guidelines in school (and elsewhere) continued to grow as the pandemic dragged on.

Ironically, the swift development of vaccines to combat the disease brought the simmering to a boil. As discussions about the potential of requiring COVID-19 vaccinations for school employees and children unfolded, many took steadfast positions on whether to get vaccinated and/or to require it of others. This situation came to a head just before the start of the 2021–2022 school year, when many schools were mostly planning to return to a "normal" school year but would require students and staff to wear masks and require vaccinations or regular testing for staff and for students wishing to participate in certain "high-risk" activities like basketball or band.

Scenes like the following played out across America: School board meetings during the summer and early fall of 2021 were inundated with parents who were furious about mask requirements and demanded that boards reconsider mandating them. It was not unusual for angry parents and community members to arrive in time for the public comments portion of the meeting and approach the microphone to share their points of view against masking and vaccination with angry arguments based on questionable research. Sometimes there was total disregard for the conventions of public commentary. Speakers would blatantly disregard signals that their allotted time was up and continue to shout above those trying to run a civil and orderly meeting. Individuals speaking in support of mask wearing and vaccinations were shouted down, mocked, and jeered. In the worst cases, police needed to be called and meetings were temporarily adjourned when some people struggled to maintain civility.

During this tumultuous time, concern over masking and vaccinations seemed to spill into other controversial topics. It was not unusual for those opposing masking to also accuse school districts, without evidence, of trying to brainwash their children by teaching critical race theory (CRT) or forcing students to learn about LGBTQ+ issues. Some parents joined together to try to have books that addressed issues of race and gender banned from school libraries. Activities planned to recognize Pride Month in June became grounds for parents to pull their children from school. Segments of communities became suspicious of efforts to promote diversity, equity, and inclusion. Those on either side of the mask and vaccination question were like the modern-day Montagues and Capulets, as were the "woke" and the "racist," the "elitist left" and the "extremist right."

As they navigated these conflicts that played out in communities, school leaders were much like the prince of Verona, trying desperately to keep the peace. In the play, the prince threatened death to any who continued to fight; he tempered this threat to mere banishment when Romeo killed Tybalt. Obviously school leaders do not have the authority to banish the adults who cannot get along. The best school leaders are able to provide a steady stream of valid, reliable, and evidence-based information to their families and staff. They provide a forum for civil discourse, and they capitalize on those moments when even those entrenched in their positions are willing to at least listen to another point of view.

If the prince of Verona could have leveraged Lord and Lady Capulet's insight into the futility of their feud with the Montagues, the play would have had a different ending. If school leaders can capitalize on those moments of consensus in their school communities, the outcomes for our students might be spared the devastating end of so many of the young people in the play. Shakespeare dramatically captures what is so often true: when adults cannot get along, young people pay the price.

Romeo and Juliet offers a few important lessons for school leaders. First, the play demonstrates that school leaders (and parents) need to know how the minds of young people work (or struggle to) and that there is a critical role for adults to explicitly develop and support students' capacity for self-control and delayed gratification. The play underscores how much impact the actions and beliefs of adults can have on children. Generations of Montagues and Capulets learned from their parents to despise the members of the other family. Students are watching the adults too. They see when their parents and school leaders are able to engage in civil discourse when they disagree—and when they don't. It is up to the adults to model good civic behavior, rational thinking, and a commitment to peace; otherwise, disaster can happen.

Perhaps the most powerful lesson from *Romeo and Juliet* is that the school leaders can learn a lot from the students they serve if they are ready to listen with an open mind. Students can tell those in charge a great deal about what matters to them, what interests and excites them and what is simply boring and pointless. This willingness to pay attention to what young people are saying requires a certain amount of humility and humanity, key characteristics of any good leader.

To summarize, here are some important leadership lessons from *Romeo and Juliet*:

1. Schools exist to serve children, so make sure you understand them and their needs. Do not waste the opportunity to shape adolescent development for the better during the period of heightened brain malleability (from ages ten to twenty-five).
2. Broaden your expectations for what school success means for each and every student. There is no one right path to success.
3. Have courage during times of divisiveness and polarization. Bravely seek to capitalize on moments of shared understanding and consensus.
4. Take time to really listen to what students have to say; their insights can be transformative.

DISCUSSION QUESTIONS

1. Are there Capulets and Montagues in your school community? That is, are there dichotomous factions of people that create divisiveness and polarization that put students' interests in harm's way? What

strategies have you used to capitalize on moments of consensus to help move the community forward?

2. What are the multiple pathways that you have made available for students who may define success in school differently—that is, those who might not plan on attending a four-year college or who pursue interests that are not traditionally offered in schools?

3. How do you help your staff strike the right balance in helping students find academic and/or behavioral success without inadvertently teaching them learned dependence?

4. "If I only knew then what I know now" may be the modern expression of what Juliet meant when she said, "Too early seen, and known too late!" What lessons do you wish you knew sooner in your educational career?

Chapter 2 will explore the tragedy of *Macbeth*, a play that offers lessons about what to do and what not to do to be a good, effective, and socially/emotionally well-balanced leader.

NOTES

1. (Steinberg 2014, 10).
2. (Steinberg 2014, 37).
3. (Steinberg 2014, 15).
4. (Positivity Project n.d.).
5. (CASEL n.d.).
6. (Steinberg 2014, 121).

BIBLIOGRAPHY

CASEL (Collaborative for Academic, Social, and Emotional Learning). Accessed September 15, 2022. https://casel.org.

Positivity Project. n.d. *The Positivity Project.* Accessed July 3, 2023. https://posproject.

Steinberg, Laurence. 2014. *Age of Opportunity: Lessons from the New Science of Adolescence.* New York: Houghton Mifflin Harcourt.

Chapter 2

Macbeth

Life's but a walking shadow, a poor player
That struts and frets his hour upon the stage
And then is heard no more. It is a tale
Told by an idiot, full of sound and fury,
Signifying nothing.

—Macbeth, Act V, Scene 5

While *Romeo and Juliet* (despite its tragic end) is filled with great quantities of love, laughter, and lightheartedness, *Macbeth* is another matter. *Romeo and Juliet* is a good starting point for school leaders to think about the children they serve who are finding their way into the world as developmental works in progress. Our youth's ever-changing minds, impetuous decision-making, and sponge-like capacity to learn are what make them such a joy to serve and support. In *Macbeth*, Shakespeare takes us to a much darker place, a place where unchecked ambition spells disaster for the title character and his wife. If *Romeo and Juliet* was a platform to explore the people school leaders serve, *Macbeth* is one that turns leaders' focus inward on themselves to explore questions about who they are as leaders and human beings.

Through the lens of the tragedy of *Macbeth*, this chapter will delve into the intersection of ambition and school leadership; the power and necessity of relationships and networks; and the quest to find social, emotional, and physical well-being as a foundation for effective and sustainable leadership. These three elements are intertwined. A key element of overall well-being that will feature prominently in this chapter is a recurring theme in *Macbeth*: the need for sleep, the often elusive elixir to the day-to-day challenges faced by all in leadership positions.

SUMMARY OF *MACBETH*

At the start of the play, Macbeth is a well-respected general in Scotland who has just fought valiantly to defeat a group of rebels who were defying the rule of King Duncan. On the way home from battle, Macbeth and his longtime close friend Banquo meet three witches who tell Macbeth that he will be the thane of Cawdor and, thereafter, king. At first, he doesn't know how either of these prophecies could be true. There already is a thane of Cawdor and a king. Before they disappear, the witches tell Banquo that he will beget kings but never be one himself.

Almost immediately, Macbeth learns that King Duncan has bestowed the title of thane of Cawdor on him to reward him for his valor and to punish Cawdor, who has been traitorous to the king. When this first of the witches' prophecies comes true, the first spark of Macbeth's ambition to be king is ignited. That spark becomes a flame when he writes to his wife, Lady Macbeth, to tell her the news. She is instantly consumed with her own desire to be queen. When she learns that King Duncan will be visiting their castle that very evening, she sees the opportunity for her husband to assume the crown. All Macbeth has to do is murder the king in his sleep.

Macbeth is initially reluctant to murder King Duncan, especially under his own roof. He has been a loyal subject and friend to his king, but Lady Macbeth spurs her husband to action by calling him a coward and questioning whether he loves her. When he asks her about what could happen if their plot fails, she says to him, "Screw your courage to the sticking place, and we'll not fail!" According to their plan, after dinner that evening, Lady Macbeth gets the king's guards intoxicated so they fall into a deep sleep, and Macbeth uses their daggers to kill the king. Macbeth is shaken by the horror of his action, so much so that he cannot complete the second part of the plan. Lady Macbeth must then return the bloody daggers to the guards to frame them for the deed.

When the murdered king and bloodied guards are discovered by the nobleman Macduff, Macbeth feigns outrage and kills the guards as an outward show of loyalty to the king, though mostly to keep them from talking and denying that they did the gruesome deed. Duncan's two sons were also at the castle, and, in fear for their own lives, they decide to flee to England. As the witches prophesied, shortly thereafter Macbeth is named king, and the downward spiral of the Macbeths' lives begins. Macbeth is wracked with guilt, which robs him of his ability to sleep. He finds that he needs to commit (or hire out) more murders in order to keep others from learning of his heinous deeds so he can keep the crown.

His next victim is his best friend, Banquo. On the day of a big feast at the palace, Banquo tells Macbeth that he and his son Fleance will go out riding before the banquet. Macbeth believes that Banquo is suspicious of him, and he sees his friend and his son as threats, particularly because the witches foretold that Banquo would not be king but would beget them. Macbeth hires some shady characters to do the deed for him, but they are only partially successful. They kill Banquo, but Fleance escapes. Macbeth is furious when his hitmen tell him that Fleance got away, but he must preside over the evening's banquet as if nothing is troubling him.

But Macbeth is troubled indeed. As all the noblemen are gathered around the table, Macbeth is rattled by a vision of Banquo's ghost, who comes to the banquet and sits in Macbeth's very seat. Macbeth struggles to keep his composure and Lady Macbeth must try to cover for his erratic behavior. When the ghost appears a second time, Macbeth is so distraught that she calls an end to the embarrassing event. That same night, Macbeth descends further into paranoia. He is worried about Macduff, the nobleman who found the body of the king and who refused Macbeth's invitation to the banquet.

Macbeth decides to consult the witches once again, and he returns to the place where his troubles all began on the moors. He finds the three "weird sisters" mixing the famous "hell broth" and chanting the well-known couplet "Double, double, toil and trouble; Fire burn and cauldron bubble." The witches conjure up three apparitions. The first tells Macbeth to "beware Macduff," the second tells him that he will never be harmed by "man of woman born," and the third assures him that he will not be vanquished until Birnam Wood advances on the castle at Dunsinane. The witches throw in one more vision before disappearing. It is the image of a long line of kings, and at the end is Banquo, fulfilling the prophecy that he would beget kings.

His visit to the witches spurs Macbeth to more action, but now his conscience no longer gives him pause as it did before he killed Duncan.

He vows that his first thoughts will be "the firstlings of my hand." His sights are set on Macduff. When he learns that Macduff has gone to England, presumably to enlist the help of Duncan's sons to remove Macbeth, Macbeth makes a move that is shocking in its heartlessness. He orders the brutal murder of Macduff's wife and children, who are home in their castle without Macduff's protection.

In the meantime, Lady Macbeth is spiraling into her own world of insanity. She, too, is unable to sleep and spends each night wandering the drafty castle, sleepwalking, and rubbing her hands together to remove the blood that she imagines is still there. Her servants observe her odd behavior and ask the doctor to try to help her. He, too, sees the incessant rubbing of her hands and hears her speaking of the deaths of Duncan, Banquo, and Macduff's children and concludes that she needs a minister or priest, not a doctor. Not long after this scene, Lady Macbeth is found dead, likely by suicide, and Macbeth is now alone, without his wife and confidant or friends.

Macduff is enraged by the murder of his family and vows to seek revenge on Macbeth. He has enlisted Duncan's sons and an army to attack the palace at Dunsinane. To disguise their numbers, Macduff directs all of the soldiers to cut branches from the trees in Birnam Wood, as camouflage. The army advances on Dunsinane, and Macbeth watches in horror as he realizes that he has been tricked by the witches: Birnam Wood is advancing on Dunsinane. Inevitably, Macbeth and Macduff meet to duel, and in a final twist of fate, Macbeth learns that Macduff was "not of woman born" but rather ripped from the womb in a version of a cesarean birth. The two battle, and Macbeth is slain. Macduff cuts off Macbeth's head and carries it to his subjects to show that Macbeth is king no more. The once noble, respected hero is vanquished and reviled. Peace returns to Scotland, but at a heavy price.

MACBETH'S TRAGIC FLAW

High school students who read *Macbeth*, or any Shakespearean tragedy, learn about the literary device called a "tragic flaw," a defect in character that brings about the downfall of the hero of a tragedy. For Macbeth and Lady Macbeth, that defect is an excessive ambition. Macbeth himself describes his flaw just before he commits his very first murder of the play when he says, "I have no spur/To prick the sides of my intent, but only/Vaulting ambition, which o'erleaps itself/And falls on the other." In other words, he has no reason to do the terrible deed, except his own ambition to be king. There is no desire to serve the people of Scotland, no calling to bring peace and prosperity to the kingdom, and no commitment to lead with wisdom and courage—just an insatiable need to have the title of king.

Those who aspire to be school and district leaders are ambitious too, and frankly, they need to be. It takes a significant amount of time, determination, and hard work to complete the educational requirements to become a certified school or district leader. There is coursework to complete, written certification exams to pass, and internships (often unpaid) to fulfill in order to gain work experience. Getting the first paid administrative position is also a challenge. Many districts are reluctant to hire new leaders who have not been fully tested by the rigors of actual administrative work. Those aspiring to make the jump to school leadership need courage to submit their applications for positions, knowing the strong likelihood of initial rejection.

School and district leaders also assume risk when they contemplate leaving the relative comfort of the classroom. No one would argue that being an effective teacher in today's classrooms is easy. It is a tremendously difficult job, but there are far more supports and protections for teachers than there are for school leaders. Teachers can be represented by strong unions and are granted certain protections under the law once they earn tenure, usually after three or four years of successful teaching. There are fewer supports and protections for school leaders. They still qualify to receive tenure after a few years of successful job performance, but union representation for school leaders is less powerful than groups that fall under the United Federation of Teachers, for example. District leaders only have the protections that they manage to negotiate into their employment contracts with boards of education. Generally speaking, superintendents work at the will of a board of education without the benefit of tenure or collective bargaining.

Superintendents are held accountable for a community's two most precious resources: children and tax dollars. This is a daunting responsibility. Not only do superintendents pledge to ensure the academic growth of their students, but they must also do everything in their power to keep the students safe from all sorts of harm and attend to their social and emotional health and wellness. This work is carried out using other people's money, and most of those "other people" do not even have children in the schools that their taxes are supporting.

School and district leaders spend a significant amount of time on the receiving end of criticism for unpopular decisions. In the current climate of divisiveness that characterizes communities, states, and the nation, almost any decision angers or offends someone. School and district leaders also regularly have to take responsibility for the inappropriate actions and errors of others and are often thrust into the media to explain what, why, and how something went wrong. It is not unheard of for school superintendents to lose their jobs over incidents that are not of their making because the school superintendent, like the CEO of a business, is ultimately responsible for everything that happens in their district, good or bad. That CEO, by the way, is likely to earn, on average, a salary that is five times higher than a superintendent. The current average salary of a CEO in the United States is $823,256.[1] The average salary for a school superintendent is $170,945.[2] So school and district leaders take on tremendous responsibility, are held directly accountable for the outcomes of their schools and districts, and do so without much of a safety net. These are all reasons why it is not unusual for those considering a school or district leadership position to be asked: Why would you want to do that?

One lesson from *Macbeth* is that ambition and its trappings are not sufficient—or even good—reasons to aspire to a leadership title. In fact, for most school and district leaders, the "why" behind their work is grounded in a genuine commitment to the care and nurture of children. The "why" must also include an understanding that leading a school or district is actually about serving a school community and all the stakeholders in it: students, teachers, staff, parents, and taxpayers.

The most effective school leaders are what Robert K. Greenleaf describes in his 1970 essay "The Servant as Leader." He says, "The servant-leader is servant first" as opposed to "leader first." Greenleaf goes on to say that servant-first leaders make sure that *other* people's highest-priority needs are being served. Key measures of the servant leader's work are answers to questions like "Do those served grow as persons? Do they, while being served, become healthier, wiser, freer, more autonomous, more likely themselves to become servants?" He also asks: What is the effect on the least privileged in that system? Will they benefit or at least not be further deprived?[3]

School and district leaders who enter their roles for the right reasons put the needs of others first and help the people they serve to develop and perform as highly as possible. From this perspective, school and district leadership is more like an answer to a calling than a quest for power or money. Mere ambition will not serve a school or district leader well. But then it didn't serve Macbeth well, either.

WOMEN WHO ASPIRE TO LEADERSHIP

Like Lady Macbeth, women who aspire to leadership climb an uphill battle, one that requires much more than ambition. Lady Macbeth is ambitious, arguably more ambitious than her husband, especially during the first half of the play. It is Lady Macbeth who is enthralled by the witches' prophecy that her husband will be king. It is Lady Macbeth who concocts the plan to kill Duncan while he is a guest in their home. It is Lady Macbeth who shames her husband into murdering Duncan using two time-tested strategies for getting men to act: accusing Macbeth of cowardice and threatening to cut him off from her love, by suggesting that he no longer loves her. In a famous soliloquy, she shares her doubts about his capacity to pursue the crown because he is too good and kind: "Yet I do fear thy nature;/It is too full o' th' milk of human kindness/To catch the nearest way."

Lady Macbeth's power over her husband is remarkable, given that the play takes place in eleventh-century Scotland, a place and time defined by its patriarchal structures in which women had little authority or legal status. Wives were expected to be subservient to their husbands. Whether rich or poor, noble or lowly, the most important role for women was that of mother and child bearer. Lady Macbeth does not fit this mold. First, Lady Macbeth is not a mother; there are no children afoot in the castle. Lady Macbeth does not seem to be bothered by the childless state of their family. In fact, she seems to revel in the strength and courage she has to follow through on the murderous plan. In another of her well-known lines, she says, "Come, you spirits/That tend on mortal thoughts, unsex me here,/And fill me from the crown to the toe top-full/Of direct cruelty." In that same speech, she goes on to say, "Come to my woman's breasts/And take my milk for gall." These lines depict a woman all too ready to give up on the role she is expected to play in exchange for a crown.

Macbeth listens to his wife and ultimately does her bidding, but it is clear that children—other people's children—are on his progressively twisted mind. He is fixated on the prophecy that Banquo will beget many kings, in stark contrast to the truth that Macbeth will beget none, and he tries to murder both father and son. Then he brutally orders the murder of Macduff's wife and children for no obvious or strategic reason other than perhaps jealousy. Sadly, in this play, none of the main characters have both a traditional happy family (with husband, wife, and children) and a position of power. Macbeth has power but no family; Macduff gets power, but his family is dead; Banquo's family comes into power, but Banquo dies before it is manifested. Does ambition for power, a call to lead, mean making a choice about having a family, or is it possible to have it all?

Women in leadership, whether in business, education, or the political arena, are still wrestling with this question more than one thousand years later. As a percentage of the total population, women lag far behind men in landing leadership positions, whether as elected officials, CEOs of corporations, or, for the purposes of this discussion, school superintendents. Even though the vast majority of teachers (74.3 percent) in US school districts are women, only a little over a quarter (28.5 percent)[4] of all school district superintendents are women, and that the number seems to slipping in the immediate aftermath of the COVID-19 pandemic, when 75 percent of women superintendents who left their position were replaced by men.[5]

For years, national- and state-level superintendent associations, along with many educational researchers, have attempted to unravel the reason behind the inverse relationship between the overall numbers of women in education and those with top leadership positions, especially since two-thirds of all leadership degrees in education are earned by women. Many theories have been considered, including the challenge of balancing a job with 24/7 expectations with the demands of family, childcare, and eldercare, which continue to fall disproportionately to women. Then there are also theories that women face a certain amount of bias during the hiring process when boards subtly (or not so subtly) exercise their worries about "family commitments" and pick men over women in a tacit nod to stereotypical gender roles in families.

Women may also lack access to some of the social networks that can lead to job opportunities and informal references that can give candidates a leg up in a search. In addition, women may put off their interests in pursuing a leadership position while they have school-age children so as to spare their children the potential strife and stress of having their mother in such a visible position on their turf. Given these gendered barriers, it is no wonder that more women leaders don't channel Lady Macbeth in frustration and say, "Unsex me here," so they have a better chance at getting the leadership job that they are willing and able to do. Ambition alone was not the answer for Lady Macbeth; she lost her mind and her life. Ambition alone will not be enough to get more women into the seats of school superintendents.

NETWORKS MATTER

Perhaps one of the most powerful cautionary lessons from *Macbeth* is how unbridled ambition can drive a person away from their most powerful sources of strength: their family, friends, and social networks. As Macbeth forces his way into being king, the once respected and revered general loses every single person who was part of his support system. He kills King Duncan, a kind man who at one time admired Macbeth and who had rewarded him for his loyalty and bravery. Macbeth hires a murderer to kill his trusted friend Banquo and his son. He has Macduff's wife and children murdered and so completes Macduff's turn against him. Macduff then recruits Duncan's son to attack and dethrone Macbeth. Other noblemen question his state of mind as they watch him hallucinate Banquo's ghost at a banquet. Little by little, everyone turns against him. By the fourth act of the play, even his wife can no longer support him, as she spirals into her own storm of guilt and insanity. His ambition isolates him so profoundly that the only resource left to him are the three witches, who clearly are not his friends and never were. His vaulting ambition does in fact overleap itself, leads to his fall, and confirms the notion that it is lonely at the top.

But it doesn't have to be. Wise leaders know that they cannot sustain themselves in their positions alone. They need to build and sustain relationships, actively seek to make connections with others, develop networks to access expertise, and have trusted colleagues who can be sounding boards and sources of help and support when needed. These are truths that apply to school leaders, especially women leaders.

One obvious way for school leaders to stay connected is to participate in opportunities to meet and talk with colleagues in formal and informal networks at the local and regional levels. One of the silver lining lessons from the COVID-19 pandemic was the power of doing just that in order to think through and problem-solve the ever-changing circumstances that upended schools during this tumultuous period. This was a time when so many questions had no clear answers: Open schools, or not? Mandate masks, or not? Require vaccinations, or not? Because the answers to these questions were fraught with controversy, vitriol, and sometimes even violence, the most successful school leaders wisely worked together with peers in neighboring districts and across regions to arrive at answers as a collective. There was a degree of "safety in numbers" for leaders on the front lines of the pandemic.

This wisdom does not need to be limited to pandemic response. Many superintendents and other school leaders saw the benefit of collaborating with their neighbors, rather than competing with them, and continued to hold regular regional meetings to talk about shared issues and challenges so as to arrive at shared solutions. The value of having a "go-to" group of colleagues became abundantly clear during this time. The truth is, everyone needs a "go-to" group in both good and bad times. Macbeth was so wrapped up in his own agenda that he did not see the value of checking in with his trusted colleagues. Imagine what would have happened if he actually spoke with Banquo or even other Scottish noblemen about the wisdom of killing Duncan in order to be king. It is likely someone would have talked him out of pursuing the crown in this manner.

The same is true for school leaders who might have a great idea to improve some aspect of their school. It is essential to share the idea, get feedback, and unearth potential barriers to the plan with many stakeholders first, before charging ahead.

Another effective way to stay connected is to join and be an active member of professional associations at the state and national levels. School and district leaders each have state and national organizations that provide many resources and varied opportunities for people to gather at leadership institutes, learning summits, and conventions. These are great ways to learn from experts in the field and colleagues. They are also places to meet others who are wrestling with similar problems or who may have discovered innovative practices to solve them. Being with other leaders from different parts of the state or nation also helps open eyes to new perspectives. These experiences can be inspiring, energizing, validating, and fun. These are all feelings that are good for the soul and sense of well-being. Macduff and Duncan's sons gathered together in England to share their perspectives on Macbeth and plan a strategy to take back the crown he effectively stole from them. Doing so ultimately resulted in ending Macbeth's bloody reign and bringing peace to the land.

It is also important for school and district leaders to build and sustain connections close to home. For school superintendents, that means thinking about and investing time in creating and sustaining a positive working relationship with the board of education. The relationship between the superintendent and the board is one that can never be taken for granted. There is an adage that the board that hires the superintendent is never the one that fires them. That's because over time, the membership on the board of education changes. Every board election can usher in new people, and even one new person creates a whole new dynamic and, in a sense, a whole new board. A superintendent cannot shortchange activities like retreats, goal setting, and plenty of regular, honest, two-way communication.

District leaders also need to think about nurturing the network among their own leadership team: the assistant superintendents, principals, assistant principals, directors, coordinators, and others who help superintendents get the work done. Wise superintendents make the cohesion of their team a priority; they encourage and reward collaboration among teammates while discouraging unhealthy competition among them. This is not always easy to do, especially when buildings or programs within a school system are vying for scarce resources, whether it be staff, time for professional development, equipment, materials, or supplies. Frequent opportunities to meet and collaborate are essential; part of the time when teams are together should focus explicitly on teamwork and an expectation for collaborative problem-solving.

Superintendents are part of this team, but they are also the person to whom everyone on that team ultimately reports, so it is critical for superintendents to strike the right balance in their relationships. They can be friendly, but not friends. They can be attentive to the personal and family challenges that touch every team member at some point, but without playing favorites; they can enjoy one another's company, but not be drinking buddies. In addition to the day-to-day rigors of running a school and a district, it is critical to take time for at least annual leadership retreats, planning time, and team building. The leadership team can and should work hard together, but they should also enjoy one another's company as human beings.

Finally, leaders must attend to the most important network of all: family. Almost all of the characters in *Macbeth* failed to pay sufficient attention to family. It could be argued that Duncan's sons did not pay enough attention to the safety of their father and he was brutally murdered in his sleep a room or two away from them at Macbeth's castle. Macduff lost both his wife and his children when he left them without sufficient protection against the murderous Macbeth, who had them killed for no reason. Macduff himself has a traumatic birth. He was "untimely ripped" from his mother's womb, a delivery we can assume took his mother's life. The Macbeths did not have any children, and while Shakespeare does not say why, one might infer that Lady Macbeth was not all that inclined to motherhood. After all, she asks the gods to turn her mother's milk to gall so that she can summon the cruelty to kill another without remorse. This plan goes poorly for her; she is wracked with guilt over her own murderous deeds.

The events of the play are extreme, but they certainly underscore the importance of keeping family at the center of one's life. Consider the contrast between Macbeth and Banquo. When Macbeth learns of his wife's death, likely by suicide, he makes one of the darkest commentaries on human life when he reduces it to "an hour upon the stage" that "signifies nothing." Banquo, by contrast, sacrificed himself in order to save his son when he and Fleance were attacked. Fleance got away, and Banquo was rewarded with creating a long line of kings!

The work of a school leader is demanding, and it can be 24/7. There are expectations that leaders will be at school, district, and community events, which translates into evening and weekend obligations tacked on to days that are already much more than 9–5. Those expectations are not likely to change. Community members want to see their school and district leaders out and about. Communities entrust their children and their resources to people who take on these leadership roles and want to know, firsthand, that they are committed and engaged. Wise leaders learn to make the most of the family time that they do have. They recognize those minutes as precious and make it a point to be fully present, not constantly checking emails, text messages, and social media. Wise and enduring school leaders make having a family dinner, at least some nights of the week or weekend, a priority. They take time to talk with their significant partners about non-work-related topics. They spend time with their children so that they know what is happening in their lives. Those moments are priceless and cannot be recouped. Just ask Macduff!

THE POWER OF SLEEP

Another important lesson from *Macbeth* is the power of sleep. After committing their murderous deeds, neither of the Macbeths can rest. They spend their nights roaming their drafty castle, tortured by their guilty consciences. In a famous scene, Lady Macbeth sleepwalks in front of both a servant and a doctor, rubbing her hands trying to remove the blood of King Duncan that she continues to "see," though it is long since washed away. After murdering the king in Act II, Scene 2, Macbeth says this about sleep:

Methought I heard a voice cry, "Sleep no more!
Macbeth doth murder sleep"—the innocent sleep,
Sleep that knits up the raveled sleeve of care,
The death of each day's life, sore labor's bath,
Balm of hurt minds, great nature's second course,
Chief nourisher in life's feast.

In other words, sleep is necessary to recover from the difficulties of the day. But how many leaders speak of (or even brag about) not sleeping like it is a badge of honor? Many leaders stay up late or get up early to get work done, often evidenced by the timestamp on the emails they have sent to colleagues or staff. Others go to bed but then cannot get to sleep or stay asleep because they are thinking about work or worrying about an upcoming meeting. Or they might be tossing and turning as they rehash in their mind an event or conflict that did not go as well as hoped. There might be a few leaders out there who really can function well without much sleep, but most people need to get sufficient rest in order to be their best, particularly over the long run. Some might be able to "get by" on a few hours of sleep a night, but that is difficult to sustain over a long career and ultimately not good for their physical or mental health. Nor is it good for leaders' families or their job performance.

Health experts recommend that adults routinely get seven to nine hours of sleep each night and list numerous negative effects when that doesn't happen over the long term. Lack of sleep for a night can leave a person tired and cranky, but long-term sleep deprivation can result in compromised short- and long-term memory, trouble with thinking and concentration, negative changes in mood, a weakened immune system, high blood pressure, weight gain, and increased risk for diabetes and heart disease. These effects are certainly not good for an individual, but they are not good for the people whom school and district leaders serve. Students, staff, and communities count on leaders to be available, calm, level-headed, patient and compassionate, and, most critically, able to make sound decisions over the long haul or in a crisis. All of this is very difficult to do when sleep deprived. The Macbeths dramatically demonstrate this point!

So the advice here: Follow the tips that we all hear about good sleep—have a routine, turn off your screens, go easy on what you eat and drink at night. Most important, always strive to do the right thing for the students you serve. When you can be confident of that, you will rest a little easier and not end up like Macbeth, getting your head handed to you, if only figuratively!

To summarize, here are some important leadership lessons from *Macbeth*:

1. Ambition is a necessary, but not sufficient, reason to become a school or district leader. The "why" must be grounded in a commitment to doing the actual work of leading and serving a school community not the desire for a title or power or money.
2. Leaders need networks of trusted colleagues at the local, regional, state, and even national level to provide inspiration, support, and camaraderie. Wise leaders devote time and effort to finding and sustaining those trusted colleagues. The need for such support and sponsorship is greater for women and leaders of color, who often face more barriers to getting and keeping top leadership positions.
3. Leaders need to establish a climate and culture of collaboration and teamwork within their own organization. It is almost impossible to make real progress when members of the team are not working together. This includes the board of education, assistant superintendents, principals, assistant principals, directors, supervisors, and non-instructional leaders.

4. Leaders need to get their rest. Leaders should not use sleeplessness as a badge of honor to prove that they are working hard. Doing so sends a message to the team that personal and family time is not valued. Lack of sleep also negatively affects physical and mental well-being, job performance, and quality of life.

DISCUSSION QUESTIONS

1. Do you know of a school or district leader who reminds you of Macbeth—that is, driven more by ambition than by a calling to do the work? What challenges do they face?
2. By the end of the play, Macbeth was isolated and alone and he darkly proclaims that "Life . . . is a tale told by an idiot, full of sound and fury, signifying nothing." One could argue that he feels this way because his motivations became corrupted with the witches promise of power. He did not have a noble "why" for his work. What is your "why" for being a school or district leader?
3. How successful are you at balancing the elements of your work and personal life and family? What strategies work for you? What are the challenges that make it difficult to strike an appropriate balance?
4. How strong and reliable is your network of trusted colleagues? To what extent can you point to individuals or groups that you can turn to for support, inspiration, and camaraderie at the local, regional, state, and national levels?
5. Do you get enough quality sleep? What steps can you take to improve your sleep habits for your own benefit and the benefit of those who live with you and those who work with you?

NOTES

1. (Chief Executive Officer Salary in the United States n.d.).
2. (School Superintendent Salary n.d.).
3. (Greenleaf 2015).
4. (School Superintendent Demographics and Statistics in the US n.d.).
5. (ILO Group 2022).

BIBLIOGRAPHY

Chief Executive Officer Salary in the United States. Accessed July 3, 2023. https://www/salary.com.

Greenleaf, Robert K. 2015. "The Servant as Leader." *The Servant as Leader.* South Orange: Center for Servant Leadership, September 29.

ILO Group. 2022. "The Superintendent Research Project: Pandemic Leadership Transitions." January 15. Accessed July 3, 2023. https://ilogroup .com>2022/02.

School Superintendent Demographics and Statistics in the US. Accessed July 3, 2023. https://www.zippia.com>demograpaphics.

School Superintendent Salary. Accessed July 3, 2023. https://salary.com.

Chapter 3

The Merchant of Venice

The quality of mercy is not strain'd,
It droppeth as the gentle rain from heaven
Upon the place beneath; it is twice blest;
It blesseth him that gives, and him that takes:
'T is mightiest in the mightiest.

—Portia, Act IV, Scene 1

The Merchant of Venice is one of Shakespeare's comedies; this means there are many love stories that unfold throughout the five acts and the ending is a happy one for almost everyone. The play is also tinged with tragedy because the central action of the play is rooted in an ancient and enduring hatred against someone who is different. Using deception, disguise, stunning wit, and clever gender role reversals, in this play Shakespeare juxtaposes themes of love and hate, generosity and greed, mercy and revenge in a tale that is ultimately about demeaning and excluding those perceived as "other." At first glance, these themes seem a poor starting point for any discussion of school and district leadership. It is hard to imagine any educational setting where hate, greed, revenge, deception, and disguise would be welcome or appropriate.

However, *The Merchant of Venice* does provide a useful lens to explore several ideas essential to effective leadership. For example, the play can be a cautionary tale about the importance of managing money and finances; it can also serve as a model for knowing and following the laws, rules, and regulations that govern school and district operations. The play can also shed some light into the importance of being savvy to the ways of the world in order to get things done, particularly if you are a woman navigating in a world that is run by men. The realm of school district leadership is, after all, still largely a man's world.

The play is also a vehicle for leaders to look inside themselves and ask what kind of leader and person they are. Do they welcome, embrace, and affirm all those who come to their schools and districts, especially those who might be perceived as "different"? Are they leaders who are generous and merciful and who keep their word? All of these essential questions are inspired and informed by this sometimes sobering comedy.

SUMMARY OF *THE MERCHANT OF VENICE*

The title character of the play is Antonio, a wealthy merchant, who has numerous ships out at sea. His best friend, the spendthrift Bassanio, needs money in order to travel to Belmont to try to win the hand of Portia, an heiress with whom he has fallen in love. Antonio is more than willing to lend his friend money, but he has little on hand while waiting for his ships to return, so Bassanio goes to Shylock, a Jewish moneylender, in order to borrow three thousand ducats. Antonio will serve as his creditor.

Shylock despises Antonio—and with good reason. Antonio, a Christian, has treated Shylock cruelly; he has spit on him and called him names. Antonio disapproves of Shylock's practice of lending money and charging interest, since at the time, around 1596, Christians were not allowed to charge interest if they loaned money to one another. However, Antonio is willing to enter into the bargain with Shylock to help his friend. Shylock looks at this situation as an opportunity to get revenge against Antonio. The bond is for three thousand ducats and would come due in three months. If Antonio forfeits on the loan, the penalty will be a pound of his flesh, taken by knife by Shylock. Because his ships are due to return in about one month, Antonio is not worried.

In the meantime, Portia is being courted by numerous suitors, none to her liking. Her deceased father established a test for each of the suitors. They had to pick one of three caskets: one made of gold, one of silver, and one of lead. The suitor that picked the right casket got to marry Portia. The first suitor, a Moor, picks the gold casket that carries an inscription saying that whoever chooses gold will get what many men desire. He is incorrect! When he opens the casket, he reads the message famously saying, "All that [glitters] is not gold," and, unceremoniously, he is asked to leave. His "suit is cold." Portia is relieved.

The second suitor, the prince of Arragon, chooses the silver casket, which says that the suitor who picks it will get as much as he deserves. This, too, is incorrect. When he opens the casket, there is no picture of Portia, just that of a "blinking fool," and he is likewise sent on his way. As these suitors are making their choices, Bassanio is on his way to Belmont to try his luck in selecting the correct casket. Portia had met Bassanio before and wants him to be correct because she is in love with him too. Bassanio picks the lead casket, which offers the warning that choosing it will require the man to "give and hazard" all he has. Ironically, it was his friend, Antonio, who had done just that for him.

While the suitors are making their choices, two important events occur in Shylock's world. First, his only daughter, Jessica, runs off to marry Lorenzo, a Christian, and she takes a great deal of his money and jewels with her. Shylock is incensed by her betrayal and perhaps even more so by the theft of his riches. Shylock then also learns that all of Antonio's ships have sunk or been overtaken by pirates, and Antonio will not be able to repay his loan. He is now fixated on getting his bond—a pound of Antonio's flesh.

When Bassanio, now married to Portia, hears the news of his friends' lost ships, he hurries back to Venice to try to help him. Portia generously offers Bassanio six thousand ducats to settle the bond, but she and her maid, Nerissa, come up with another plan to save Antonio. They, too, race off to Venice, disguised as learned men, a judge and a clerk, to argue in court on Antonio's behalf.

In the courtroom where Antonio has resigned himself to his doomed fate, Portia, posing as an attorney named Balthasar, begins her argument with a plea to Shylock to show mercy on Antonio in one of the loveliest and most well-known passages of the play: "The quality of mercy is not strain'd/It droppeth as the gentle rain from heaven/Upon the place beneath." Shylock is unmoved by her reflection on mercy and demands to have his bond; he insists that the court follow the "letter of the law." Portia then pivots to her argument that grants both of his requests, and it proves to be Shylock's undoing. She reasons that Shylock can indeed have his pound of flesh; Antonio did not pay in time and that was the deal. However, in taking that pound of flesh, Shylock cannot shed even a drop of blood, since there was no mention of blood in the bond. And he must take care to take exactly one pound of flesh as was stated in the bond. To go even a hair over would mean that he violated the agreement and would forfeit the deal. Shylock knows this is impossible and he has been outsmarted. Shylock is bereft. After some back and forth between the duke (who presided over the trial) and Antonio, it is determined that Shylock must give half of his money to the state and the other half in a trust to his daughter and her Christian husband. And Shylock must become a Christian. Shylock leaves the courtroom in despair, saying, "I am not well." This is a profound understatement.

Not satisfied with her triumph over Shylock, Portia and her maid, Nerissa, still disguised, decide to test their husbands. When they each wed, they gave their new husbands a ring to symbolize their love, and each husband vowed to never remove the ring from their finger. However, after the trial, Bassanio is so appreciative of "Balthasar's" winning argument that he wants to repay him in some way. Portia asks for the ring. After trying to explain why he can give anything except the ring, Bassanio reluctantly relents. Gratiano, Nerissa's husband, does the same. The play concludes with the two women verbally teasing their husbands for giving up their rings so easily and then revealing that it was the two of them in disguise who saved the day. Portia and Bassanio, Nerissa and Gratiano, Jessica and Lorenzo live happily ever after. Even Antonio's ships return safely; they were not lost at sea after all. Only Shylock is ruined. He lost his daughter, his money, his bond, and his religion.

MONEY MATTERS

The Merchant of Venice is filled with cautionary tales about the management (or mismanagement) of money that can be instructive to those who are or aspire to be school or district leaders. The task of leading school financial matters is often cited by aspiring leaders to be the area in which they feel least prepared and that worries them most when contemplating making a career move to school administration, especially at the district level. There is good reason for that worry, too. Managing district finances is an enormous part of the job, first and foremost because, without sound financial footing, schools cannot deliver on their mission to appropriately educate children, and second because the money that is being managed is "other people's." Taxpayers can and do hold school district leaders accountable for poor money management by defeating budgets, voting out board members, or demanding the removal of top administrators.

There are plenty of examples of *what not to do* with money in *The Merchant of Venice*. First, there is Bassanio, who by station in life should have the resources to travel to Belmont and "make a good showing" as a suitor to the heiress Portia. However, Bassanio has spent all of his money frivolously. He admits that he has "disabled [his] estate" with his "prodigal" ways, and he must ask Antonio to take a chance on him by loaning him money to win Portia. His explanation for why Antonio should help him is quite remarkable. He compares his request for money to a time in his youth when after losing one arrow, he would shoot another in the exact same direction with the hope of finding both. Fortunately for Bassanio, Antonio does not equate that thinking with throwing good money after bad and generously agrees to help him. It is Bassanio's hope that money borrowed from Antonio will make it possible for him to marry the wealthy Portia and so he will be set for life. So in sending another "arrow" Bassanio's way, he (and Antonio) will recoup previous losses and then some!

Imagine what would happen if school district leaders managed money in this way? While public school leaders can predict with certainty that a steady stream of students will show up each and every fall expecting a free and appropriate education, the funding for schools is not as steady or predictable. The revenue that supports public education is subject to the ups and downs of the economy, the capacity of a community to levy sufficient tax dollars, and, at the federal level, the changing priorities of the political party in power. On the expenditure side, public schools are also affected by costs that generally only go up: contractual salary increases, employee benefits (including health insurance), energy and fuel costs, and increased costs in everything from school buses to printer cartridges. Therefore, it is wise for school leaders to use financial management strategies that are as steady and predicable as possible.

This is easier to say than it is to do. When times are good, the economy is strong, state aid is flowing freely, and federal dollars are available, there is tremendous pressure on school leaders to spend those resources on things that no one can easily argue against: lower class sizes, specialized staff to help students who struggle, updated technology, additional school security, and more. Problems arise when the inevitable economic downturn arrives and districts have added items that need continued funding after the revenue that supported them either goes away or remains flat. That is when difficult decisions must be made and when school leaders can become hugely unpopular—or worse. Shakespeare doesn't say exactly what Bassanio squandered his money on, and it may not exactly matter if he spent it on noble causes or frivolous wants. The point of the play is that he didn't have it when he needed it most, and that reality put himself and his friend in peril. It is children and taxpayers who are put in educational peril when school and district leaders manage their resources using the Bassanio school of thought.

Antonio, the title character, is also a poor role model for school and district leaders. He announces at the start of the play that he is sad and weary for reasons neither he nor his friends can pinpoint, but one theory is that he is worried about his many ships that are all out at sea at once. Antonio is deeply entrenched in the vibrant trade activity centered in the Rialto, the economic heart of Venice, a city that was itself an economic hub for trade in Europe, Asia, and the Far East during the sixteenth century. Antonio shows himself to be a huge risk taker, more than a little overconfident, and, at least when it comes to the moneylender Shylock, quite arrogant. Antonio has stretched himself so thin financially, waiting for his ships to come in, that when an unanticipated expense arises (Bassanio's request), he does not have the resources to address it. He must borrow money at an interest rate that literally puts his life in jeopardy.

There is a lot wrong with how Antonio does business. Why risk all of his wealth at one time? The safety of sailing vessels during this time was far from guaranteed. Bad weather, treacherous passageways, and unscrupulous pirates were all real threats to ships traversing the seas. Antonio is hopeful that because he has diversified his interests by sending ships in many different directions, his fortunes will ultimately be safe, but at least until the very end of the play, when miraculously all is well, he and Shylock believe that all of his ships are lost. If Antonio did not "risk and hazard all," like the inscription on the lead casket said, he would have had the money to loan to Bassanio and would not have had to deal with Shylock.

Public school and district leaders cannot let all of their ships go out to sea at once either. They need to have a robust savings account so that when the inevitable unexpected need emerges, there are funds available to address it, without having to borrow money at greater taxpayer expense.

Shylock also has a misguided view of how to manage money. He is a moneylender by trade, but perhaps not by choice. For hundreds of years, including the time when Shakespeare wrote this play, Jews were associated with moneylending, in part because they were prohibited from owning land or participating in trade guilds and needed to find other ways to make a living. As far back as medieval times, Christian theology taught that charging interest on a loan was a sin, so few Christians entered this line of work, and therefore many Jews engaged in financial transactions as a livelihood. Shylock, however, seems to be excessively fixated on his money and other possessions.

When he learns that his only daughter, Jessica, has run off with a Christian, he is furious, but it is hard to tell whether he is angrier at her for abandoning him, leaving his religion, or taking a significant amount of his money and jewels. He is reported saying, "My daughter! O my ducats! O my daughter!/Fled with a Christian! O my Christian ducats!/ Justice! The law!" Shylock, a widower, seems to believe that all that glitters is indeed gold and has lost sight of the importance of having his only remaining family member close to him. For her part, Jessica states that her house with Shylock is "hell" and that she is "ashamed to be her father's child" because of his manner of doing business and obsession with money.

There will be much more to say about Shylock, but one lesson that school and district leaders can take from him is the warning that being too interested in the financial side of leading a school district and not sufficiently committed to the mission of serving children can be disastrous. Shylock's obsession with money cost him his daughter. A similar obsession by school leaders could result in shortchanging opportunities for students in exchange for an excessive interest in stockpiling savings. Having too many savings tucked away can also anger the very people who funded those savings: taxpayers! Balancing mission and money, while respecting the community who pays the bill, is the essence of good financial stewardship.

THE LETTER OF THE LAW

It takes a great deal more than a love of children and expertise in the field of teaching and learning in order to be an effective school or district leader. A leader also needs to know how things work in the legal, political, and social realms of the job. Just as Antonio's ships needed to navigate some rough seas and equally rough characters on their way to port, so, too, do school leaders sometimes have to navigate some perilous obstacles in the real world.

Portia is an excellent, if sometimes ironic, role model for skillful navigation of the "rules" of engagement in life—excellent because she gets exactly what she wants and needs by the end of the play through playing by the rules, and ironic because she sometimes has to pretend to be something that she is not in order to so.

One example is how she manages to marry the man she actually loves while honoring the rules established by her deceased father. In the sixteenth century, young women (especially those from wealthy families) rarely got the chance to marry a person of their choosing; most often it was their fathers who got to make the choice. Portia was indeed the heiress of her father's wealth, but even from the grave he wanted control over who she married and how that wealth would be managed. He ostensibly took that decision out of Portia's hands by devising the test of the gold, silver, and lead caskets from which suitors would choose.

Portia dutifully submitted to the process and followed her father's rules with the suitors but not without her own subtle agency. After rejecting many suitors before they even had the opportunity to guess the proper casket, she gave two suitors, the Moor and the prince of Arrogon, the opportunity to choose. In the brief time, she interacted with each, she knew they were not the match for her and was obviously relieved when they chose incorrectly and had to depart. But when Bassanio arrived to make his choice, Portia took action to make sure he picked the lead casket. She was already in love with him and wanted him to be successful. As Bassanio contemplated which casket to select, Portia arranged to have musicians perform a song, where many of the lyrics rhymed with lead: "Tell me where is fancy bred/Or in the heart or in the head?/It is engender'd in the eyes/With gazing fed." Whether it was these subtle hints or Bassanio's capacity to see beyond the superficial beauty of the gold and silver caskets, he made the right choice, and the couple were blissfully married. Portia was able to follow the rules and not leave the outcome entirely to chance.

But her role in guiding Bassanio to the lead casket was just the warm-up for her brilliance in knowing and using the rules in order to save his friend Antonio from sure death at the hands of Shylock. Disguised as a man and armed with some legal expertise she gleaned from her wise cousin, Doctor Bellario, Portia and her maid race to Venice to square off with Shylock in a court of law. As women, Portia and Nerissa would have no right to be present in a court of law, much less allowed to make a legal argument. And beyond the disguise, both need to lie about their whereabouts to their friends minding their home in Belmont. Portia and Nerissa claim they will be at a nearby monastery praying for Antonio's safekeeping and Bassanio's return. Again, Portia understands the rules of engagement in sixteenth-century Italy, and she uses those rules to save the day, something none of the male characters in the play seem able to do.

Similarly, effective school and district leaders, while bound to follow all sorts of rules, regulations, and laws established by others, cannot sit idly by when students' needs are not being met or when those rules and regulations actually disadvantage some (or all) students. There are numerous areas in education where the rules can get in the way of good practice in education.

For example, starting with our youngest learners, there are federal dollars to support free "universal" pre-kindergarten programs. Purportedly, the money would support children and families most in need of early education, but because seats in programs are scarce, all children are placed into a lottery system, so any eligible four-year-old child may get placed. What often happens is that families who do not need assistance get a seat by lucky chance, and poorer families, also by chance, are out of luck. No one disputes the value of early education; all young children will benefit from the opportunity to learn and play with peers in an age-appropriate, well-staffed setting, but it is disheartening to know that children of low-income families who need access most are at the mercy of a lottery. It is also difficult to watch privileged families, who would provide the experience regardless, get a free ride at the expense of others. School and district leaders have a moral obligation to bring these failed rules to the attention of those who make them.

Another example involves hiring qualified teachers. A tangle of certification requirements, which vary by state, can also be a barrier to hiring an individual who is best suited to teach a particular grade or subject. Finding talented and committed teachers to fill open positions has always been a real challenge for school and district leaders. That challenge has become even more daunting since the COVID-19 pandemic upended schools and teaching and learning, leaving students with gaps in their academic and social/emotional development. Teachers are burning out, leaving the profession in droves because the work has become so difficult, especially in school districts that serve communities with high levels of poverty and children of color. According to the National Center for Educational Statistics, 44 percent of public schools had teacher vacancies at the start of the 2022 school year. Other reports predict that 75 percent of schools nationwide will experience shortages.[1] Yet states' certification requirements, purportedly established to confirm teacher qualifications, are often so convoluted and restrictive that they contribute to the difficulty of hiring and retaining teachers, particularly in areas like special education, world languages, technology education, and the sciences. Students pay the ultimate price when there is not a high-quality, motivated, and committed teacher guiding their learning. Like the pre-kindergarten dilemma, school and district leaders need to advocate for sensible certification requirements with their state education departments.

There are many other aspects of public education that are laden with well-intended rules, regulations, and laws meant to protect the interests of children, covering everything from how school communities build their facilities, transport children, feed children, provide medical services, serve students with disabilities, and discipline students who violate conduct codes, to name just a few. Not unlike the rules and procedures that Portia's father established to protect her and her inherited wealth, those rules can and do complicate the end in mind: for Portia to marry the person she loves, and for school and district leaders to serve their children and community well. The point here is not that rules, laws, and regulations should be abolished; rather, leaders need to know them inside and out so that they can successfully follow them (as all school leaders are sworn to do) and, when necessary, advocate to those who make those rules at the local, state, and national levels to alter them. In other words, school and district leaders need to take a page out of Portia's book: be smart, be bold, and be committed to your cause. In the twenty-first century, let's hope female leaders don't need to pretend to be men to do so.

TREATING "OTHERS"

The most sobering aspect of *The Merchant of Venice* is the treatment of individuals who are not white, wealthy, male, or Christian. Women need to dress as men in order to be seen or heard in a court of law; Portia's future marriage is a kind of "let's make a deal" game show set up by her deceased father; Jessica must sneak off to be with the Christian man she loves. The only black character in the play, "The Moor," knows that his dark skin could be off-putting to the fair Portia. His first spoken words in the play are "Mislike me not for my complexion." And when he chooses incorrectly, Portia is relieved and then dismisses all who might be dark skinned: "A gentle riddance. Draw the curtains go./ Let all of his complexion choose me so." Those without wealth or station in society are minor characters who are not taken seriously, playing the roles of fools offering comic relief. But no other person in the play is treated with more contempt, disdain, and hatred than Shylock the Jew.

Shakespeare did not likely know any Jewish people since they were banned from England from the late thirteenth century until the middle of the seventeenth century, but he was likely aware of Jews living in Venice, Italy. He was also likely aware of an Italian play by Ser Giovanni Fiorentino called *Il Pecorone* that tells a tale very similar to *The Merchant of Venice*.[2]

Jews had been living and working in Venice for centuries, but in the early 1500s they successfully negotiated with city leadership to own land in their own quarter called the "Ghetto."[3] The Ghetto was a tiny section of the city where Jews could establish permanent residence and build their synagogues and community. The Ghetto in Venice was a cosmopolitan center; Jews from all over Europe relocated there to live, work, and worship. And as more and more people moved there, the only way for the Ghetto to grow was to build upward; thus, it is known as one of the first "vertical" cities. However, the Ghetto was still a place where Jews were segregated from the rest of the citizens of Venice; in fact, the gates of the Ghetto were locked each night, so the Jews could not travel freely around the city after nightfall. Additionally, when doing business in the rest of the city, Jews were required to wear a yellow hat or a yellow badge on their clothing so other Venetians would know their heritage. The horror that Jews faced in Nazi Germany under Hitler leading up to and during World War II had roots going back centuries. Sadly, anti-Semitism continues to rear its head well into the twenty-first century.

Shakespeare played on all of the negative stereotypes of the Jewish moneylender, perhaps because it would have resonated with his audience at the time. What is not clear is whether Shakespeare actually subscribed to those stereotypes. Shylock speaks one of the most famous passages of the play (and arguably among all of Shakespeare's plays) when he points out that he is no different from any other human being:

> I am a Jew. Hath not a Jew eyes? Hath not a Jew hands, organs, dimensions, senses, affections, passions? fed with the same food, hurt with the same weapons, subject to the same diseases, healed by the same means, warmed and cooled by the same winter and summer, as a Christian is? If you prick us, do we not bleed? if you tickle us, do we not laugh? if you poison us, do we not die? and if you wrong us, shall we not revenge?

Shylock is like every other human being: flawed. Flawed, just like the Christians who spat on him, insulted him, and forbade him to participate in almost all forms of enterprise or own land outside the Ghetto. Those same Christians prevented him from almost all enterprises except lending money and scorned him because he charged interest on those loans, even though it was one of the few ways he could actually earn an income to support his family. These are the same wealthy Christians who during the sixteenth century on the Rialto had a robust slave trade of people of all ages and races to perform the mundane labors of the day. So it is not all that surprising that Shylock is without mercy in collecting on his bond with Antonio. He is put in a position where it is almost impossible to "win," and by the end of the play, he does in fact lose everything.

So what is the lesson from Shylock for school and district leaders when it comes to serving each and every child, especially those children who might be considered "other" in some way? Schools and districts across the United States are filled with students who can feel "othered" by their school environment, the curriculum they are expected to learn, their access to learning opportunities, the collection of books in their libraries, the school calendar they follow, and so much more. Students of color, students with disabilities, students who are LGBTQ+, students who are economically disadvantaged, students whose first language is not English, and students who practice religions that are not Christianity can all find themselves in schools and classrooms where they do not see themselves reflected and do not feel like they are seen, heard, affirmed, or valued. This is an enormous failure of mission if school and district leaders are truly committed to serving each and every child. Too many schools are falling short of providing an equitable learning experience to all of our children.

Sadly, many of the children who can feel as if they are "other" in their schools can feel the effects in a wide variety of destructive ways. Students who do not feel like they are welcome in their own schools, who do not feel a sense of inclusion and belonging in their classrooms, are often the students who underachieve academically, are disproportionately classified as having a disability, are disproportionately referred for discipline, are the victims of bullying, have poor attendance, or experience one of a number of other measures that indicate a student is struggling in school. When one looks at this situation critically, it truly is no wonder that many students are not finding success and happiness at school. How can we expect anyone, at any age, to find joy and fulfillment in their work (or school) when they do not feel like they belong? Could anyone expect Shylock to be a kind, generous, forgiving individual when he was treated as an outcast who was unable to live where he wanted, engage in any profession he wanted, and practice his religion freely?

Shylock's reminder that Jews bleed when they are pricked, laugh when they are tickled, and die when they are poisoned is the reason for readers of the play to have some empathy for this human being, even though he gets little empathy or sympathy in the play. Not only do school and district leaders need to have empathy for the students and families they serve who may feel like "others" in their school community, but they must also take action to right those wrongs and ensure that each and every student has an equitable—not equal—shot at success in schools. To be equitable, school and district leaders must provide each and every student with what they need, which is not the same as giving all students the same thing. There are some students who will need specialized instruction to help them access the curriculum because they have a learning disability; there are others who will need extra help to become readers. There are students who will need help learning English as a new language. To be equitable, each and every student needs something a little different to have full access to the opportunities that a school offers. One size, one equal size, does not fit all students.

In recent years, there has been a growing urgency among many school and district leaders to pursue equity for the children they serve. The commitment to the work around cultural proficiency is taking hold. It has become a top priority for several (but not all) state education departments around the nation. Numerous school districts seek to recognize and affirm diversity as a cherished part of our national heritage. Many educational leaders are taking bold action to pursue true inclusion in their school buildings and districts by looking at their work through the lens of equity. This effort means asking questions like the following: Do the demographics of our teachers reflect those of our students? Which of our students have access to our higher-level courses? Who are the students who are suspended most and for what? Does our curriculum include meaningful reference to the diversity of our students? Is global history truly global or mostly European centered? Does US history include the full story of America, including the unsavory story of slavery? Do our science, English, art, music, and other curricula include the stories and accomplishments of women, people of color, and those with disabilities?

These and a thousand more questions like them make some people very uncomfortable. As school and district leaders take up the work of diversity, equity, and inclusion, some communities have taken offense and have pushed back, particularly when schools take on issues related to race and racism and the LGBTQ+ community. This pushback has taken many forms, from accusations that schools are teaching "critical race theory" as a means of making white children feel bad about their privileged status in our culture, to campaigns to censor books from school libraries, to hotly contested school board elections in which candidates run on a platform of "taking back our schools" by exerting pressure on decisions related to curriculum, budget priorities, and hiring. All of these measures are an attempt to maintain a school environment that affirms the white, middle-class, Christian, cisgender, ableist, heterosexual experience to the marginalization of all other experiences.

Even though it is doubtful that any K–12 school district is teaching "critical race theory" (an academic concept that is typically explored in the realm of graduate-level legal studies), the hue and cry against it has upended civil discourse at board meetings, put DEI initiatives on hold, and cost some school and district leaders their jobs. The work around equity and cultural proficiency is not for the faint of heart, and yet it is work that must be done if school leaders truly care about the children they serve.

THE QUALITY OF MERCY AND
THE VALUE OF YOUR WORD

Portia, disguised as a learned (and male) attorney, offers one of the most beautiful tributes to the quality of mercy in her opening argument with Shylock, who is ready to take his literal pound of flesh from Antonio. In that speech, she says that mercy is an attribute of God himself and that when those on earth show mercy, they are very much like

God. She also points out that everyone on earth will eventually plead for mercy from God, and not justice, because all individuals are flawed and need salvation. Despite her impassioned speech, there is no mercy in this play. Shylock is not inclined to show mercy; he wants his bond. Portia does not show mercy to Shylock either, catching him in his own trap of following the letter of the law. Likewise, the duke and his court show little mercy to Shylock, taking away his wealth and requiring him to convert to Christianity. So whether or not Shakespeare himself subscribed to the transformative power of mercy, none of his characters do in the end.

School and district leaders need to take their advice from Shakespeare's words and not his characters' actions. Although a certain amount of power and authority does rest with school and district leaders (though far less than one would think), they do have the power to be kind and compassionate and to give grace and show mercy to the people within the school community they serve. This does not mean that school and district leaders should not hold students, staff, and others accountable for repeated infractions of codes of conduct, patterns of poor job performance, or worse. Leaders have the obligation to keep their school buildings safe and to ensure that quality teaching and learning are underway, so there are times when consequences are necessary for the greater good. However, all decisions and actions can be infused with an understanding of the quality of mercy, a recognition of the humanity of each person within a school community, including the school leader. They are human too.

Finally, the play ends with Portia and Nerissa testing the promises that each of their husbands made when they married to never remove or give away their wedding rings. However, both Bassanio and Graziano give over their rings to the learned team who saved their friend Antonio, albeit not knowing that the "men" are in fact their wives. Portia and Nerissa chide their husbands unmercifully for a time before revealing their identity and the reality that their husbands did not in fact give the rings to others. The two are humbled and relieved when it all works out in the end.

The final lesson for school and district leaders here is to be sure to treat your word as if it is a precious ring, because it is. There is nothing that can undermine the capacity to lead more than failing to keep your word in matters both big and small. People have a way of remembering what you have promised and what you have said and have an expectation that a leader of integrity will be as good as their word.

To summarize, here are some important leadership lessons from *The Merchant of Venice*:

1. Learn how to be a responsible steward of the school or district's resources. This is an essential obligation for schools and especially district leaders, for which they will be held accountable.
2. Learn the rules of engagement for leading your school or district. Leaders must understand and follow the laws and regulations that govern their organizations; leaders must also know how and when to advocate to have those laws and regulations amended when they do not serve children well.
3. Be courageous and creative when problem-solving on behalf of children, tempered by lessons #1 and #2 above!
4. Celebrate the diversity of your students and staff; embrace and affirm each and every person for who and what they are, particularly those who are in historically marginalized groups.
5. Be a leader who keeps their word; don't promise things that you might not be able to deliver.
6. Show mercy to those who need it. Being a strong leader does not mean that you do not have compassion for the human beings who make up your school community.
7. Leaders are human too. They bleed when pricked and laugh when tickled. Embrace your own and others' humanity.

DISCUSSION QUESTIONS

1. What groups in your school community might feel like they do not fully belong? How do you know? Are there structures (policies, procedures, traditions) in place that cause or reinforce the exclusion of some groups from full participation in all that your school or district offers? What can you do as an individual to welcome and affirm each and every student in your schools? What can you do to make sure that your school or district has systems in place that prevent some members of the school community from feeling "othered" and excluded?

2. In *The Merchant of Venice*, women save the day, but they have to pretend to be men to do so. To what extent do you believe that women in school leadership today need to don a mantle of masculinity in order to be hired as a school district leader? To have longevity as a school district leader? To be effective as a school district leader who must make difficult and sometimes unpopular decisions?

3. School and district leadership can be complicated by the natural tension that exists between needing to follow laws, regulations, policies, collective bargaining agreements, codes of conduct, and so on, and the reality that the business of school is all about people: children, their parents, and employees who have complicated lives outside of the school environment. It is sometimes difficult to balance the demands of doing things right ("by the book") with doing the right thing for the human beings involved and granting a little mercy. Think of a time when you or a leader you know wrestled with this dilemma. How did you or your colleague decide the best course of action? What was the outcome? Would you or your colleague do the same thing again?

4. Do you know of some rules or regulations, policies, or procedures that are holding your organization back from achieving its stated goals? What steps can you take to change the things that are holding your organization back from serving students well?

NOTES

1. (Elias and DeLaRosa 2022).
2. (Royal Shakespeare Company n.d.).
3. (Worrall 2015).

BIBLIOGRAPHY

Elias, James, and Josue DeLaRosa. 2022. *U.S. Schools Report Increased Teacher Vacancies Due to COVID-19 Pandemic, New NCES Data Show.* Press Release. Washington: National Center for Educational Statistics. Accessed July 4, 2023. https://nces.ed.gov/whatsnew/press_releases/3_3_2022.asp.

Royal Shakespeare Company. n.d. *Dates and Sources.* Accessed July 4, 2023. https://www.rsc.org.uk.dates-and-sources.

Worrall, Simon. 2015. *The Centuries-Old Hisotry of Venice's Jewish Ghetto.* Special Report. *Smithsonian Magazine.* https://www.smithsonianmag.com/travel/venice-ghetto-jews-italy-anniversary-shaul-bassi-180956867.

Chapter 4

Julius Caesar

For I have neither wit, nor words, nor worth,
Action, nor utterance, nor the power of speech,
To stir men's blood: I only speak right on;
I tell you that which you yourselves do know.

—Mark Antony, Act III, Scene 2

Shakespeare's *Julius Caesar* is a timeless—and true—story about political power. It includes all of the trappings of classic power struggles, including conspiracy, tyranny, persuasion, and punishment, which is why it has been a staple of the high school classroom for so long. The play is also the source of numerous expressions that have found their way into the modern-day vernacular. "Beware the ides of March," "Et tu Bruté?" and "Friends, Romans, countrymen, lend me your ears" are just a few expressions that almost anyone is able to quote, even if they do not know the source. Also attributable to the play are the familiar ideas of "falling on the sword" when all is lost and of "climbing the career ladder" and leaving former friends and peers behind (or below). *Julius Caesar* is an iconic but relatively short play. It is also an unusual play in that the title character dies early in the third act, killed by conspirators who fear that he will use his unfettered power to become a tyrant.

There are many reasons why it is worthwhile for high school students to learn about *Julius Caesar*, but there are even more reasons why it is an effective teaching tool for those who lead the schools and districts where those students go to study and learn. From Caesar, leaders can learn invaluable lessons about the power of persuasive speech, the wisdom of listening, and the prudence to know how and when to do each. The play also provides insight into why leaders need a healthy dose of humility and why they must recognize their own fallibility. Caesar believed his judgment was beyond reproach and that he could bask in his popularity among the people to be and do whatever he wanted. This, of course, was not true, and it cost him his life. For school and district leaders, such character flaws may not cost them their lives, but they could cost them their livelihoods!

SUMMARY OF *JULIUS CAESAR*

The action of *Julius Caesar* begins on the streets of Rome in the early days of March 44 BC with commoners waiting for their opportunity to see the title character. Caesar is a powerful general and crafty politician and the supreme leader of the Roman Empire. The gathered fans of the immensely popular Caesar know he is on his way through town to watch the races. As they wait, they sing the praises of their great leader. Soon Caesar and his entourage pass by, and a man known to be a soothsayer shouts to Caesar the first of many famous lines from the play: "Beware the ides of March!" Caesar quickly, and unwisely, dismisses the warning as irrelevant to him and continues on his way.

Shortly thereafter two of Caesar's old friends, Brutus and Cassius, reflect on Caesar's rise to power. Brutus is an honorable man with a long and dignified pedigree of ancestors who were deeply committed to the city of Rome and its republican practices. Brutus loves Caesar and Rome, and his central dilemma in the early scenes of the play is to decide which he loves more. Cassius has also known Caesar since they both were very young, and he is profoundly jealous of Caesar's meteoric rise to power and popularity. In speaking with Brutus, Cassius reminisces about instances when Caesar was not so mighty and needed Cassius to save him, once when Caesar nearly drowned during some youthful horseplay and another when Caesar begged him for care when was sick with fever. Capitalizing on Brutus' profound love of Rome, Cassius plants the seeds of doubt in Brutus' mind. According to Cassius, if no action is taken, Caesar, already godlike in the minds of the common people, will let his power go to his head and become a tyrant.

In the meantime, Cassius is recruiting other conspirators to assist in the assassination of Caesar. He knows that if the well-respected and trusted Brutus approves of the plot and assists in its execution, other prominent Romans will approve as well. Cassius also orchestrates the delivery of letters to Brutus' home that fabricate stories of Caesar's tyranny. All of the letters are written in different handwriting so that Brutus begins to believe that concerns about Caesar's intentions and actions are widespread throughout the city. Brutus struggles mightily with his decision to join in with the conspirators. He is restless and agitated and unable to sleep. His wife Portia, also of a noble Roman family, cannot help but notice his distress and begs him to tell her what is troubling him. He promises to share all of his secret musings with her after she promises that she will never tell his secrets.

As Brutus struggles to determine his course of action, he reflects on the story he heard about what happened when Caesar was at the races. While there, the people offered Caesar a crown, not once or twice but three times; three times he turned it down, not out of humility but to further arouse the people. On top of that, Brutus worries about the stories told in the letters he received about Caesar's potential tyranny. In the end, Cassius' unrelenting insinuations against Caesar are persuasive, and Brutus is convinced, without legitimate evidence, that it is the right and noble thing to assassinate his friend Caesar. The date and time of the assassination are set for 8:00 a.m. on March 15, the ides of March.

A terrible storm rages through Rome the night before the assassination plot is to unfold. There is terrifying thunder and lightning and stories of graves opening up, spilling the dead, and wild animals roaming the streets. Caesar's wife, Calpurnia, is disturbed by the weather and frightened by an unsettling dream she had that features a bleeding statue of Caesar; she begs her husband not to go to the Senate as planned. Initially he agrees to stay with her, but then Decius enters and tells Caesar that he must report to the Capitol. The Senate is poised to crown him, and besides, Caesar would be mocked without mercy if he failed to show up because of his wife's worry and fear over a bad dream. Little does Caesar know that Decius is one of the conspirators. Caesar reports to the Capitol and, within moments of arriving, is confronted by the conspirators and stabbed to death but not before seeing his dear, former friend among them and saying, "Et tu, Bruté?"

The assassination sends Rome into chaos and sets the stage for Mark Antony to deliver one of the most famous and politically astute speeches ever. Mark Antony is a true friend of Caesar, so true a friend that Cassius wanted to assassinate him too. But Brutus would not allow it. Rather, Mark Antony is to deliver the eulogy for Caesar, which has the purpose of rallying Caesar's loyalists to seek revenge, though without giving the conspirators any reason to believe that he is doing just that. At the conclusion of Antony's remarks, an angry mob is riled up to kill the conspirators. Brutus and Cassius flee Rome, and a bloody, violent civil war ensues.

The final two acts of the play tell of the downward spiral of Cassius and Brutus against Caesar's loyal subjects, led by Mark Antony. Cassius and Brutus each lead their own armies, and they are supposed to be working together, but their communication with each other is poor and they cannot agree on their military strategy. They argue about who is the better soldier and who cares more about the other. During a particularly fraught discussion, Brutus learns that his wife Portia has taken her own life in a most unusual way. She has "swallowed fire"—that is, she put a burning coal in her mouth and held it there until she choked to death, presumably to show that even in her deep despair, she would not divulge Brutus' conspiratorial secrets, just as she promised.

Like Macbeth, Brutus finds it almost impossible to sleep while the war he caused rages on. On one particular night, he asks a young musician to serenade him while he tries to read, but rather than falling asleep, he is visited by the ghost of Caesar. The visit is short but ultimately confirms Brutus' fate. Caesar says, "Thou shalt see me at Philippi." This is the place where Cassius and Brutus finally decided they would battle next.

Meanwhile, on the plains of Philippi, Mark Antony and Octavius (Caesar's grandnephew) get word that Brutus and Cassius are advancing for battle, and they are delighted that their foes are bringing the battle to them, rather than the other way around. Before the battle, Cassius and Brutus say their goodbyes, recognizing that this battle will end the war they began on the ides of March. A fierce battle is fought, but once again a miscommunication causes confusion. Cassius wrongly believes that his army is surrounded by Mark Antony's troops, and he takes his own life with the same sword that killed Caesar. Cassius would rather be dead than have to enter the city of Rome as a captive prisoner of war.

Brutus finds the body of his friend Cassius, and a sense of dread falls on him too. As the battle continues throughout the day, one after another of his men are killed, and Brutus sees the inevitability of his own demise. Rather than await death at the hands of Mark Antony and his men, he asks a servant to hold his sword. Brutus then takes his own life by literally falling on the sword. At the end of the play, Mark Antony finds the body of his foe and finds it impossible to despise him. Until the end, in his eyes, Brutus was a man of honor and courage, but one who was tragically misled.

LISTENING AND SPEAKING REIGN SUPREME

If ever there was a story to illustrate how much words matter, the tragedy of *Julius Caesar* is it. The fate of almost every character in this story is the result of the spoken word. Words can honor, persuade, and inspire; they can also manipulate, insinuate, and confuse. The winners and losers in this play are determined by those who effectively speak *and listen* to the words of others and those who do not. Effective (and not so effective) school and district leaders are determined the same way. This chapter will explore what it means to be an effective speaker and listener, starting with the latter because, as the lead characters in *Julius Caesar* illustrate, the failure to listen, more so than a failure to speak, ultimately determines their fate.

Julius Caesar was a poor listener, especially when the words came from those without status in 44 BC Rome: commoners, "soothsayers," and women! Though historical accounts of Caesar's life mention nothing of deafness, Shakespeare underscored this weakness literally by making him deaf in his left ear. He has Caesar say to his friend Antony as they walk along in Act II, "Come on my right hand, this ear is deaf." Whether physically impaired or simply too arrogant to listen, Caesar summarily dismissed the words of many. The first example was the warning of the "fortune-teller" who told him to beware of the ides of March. He also ultimately dismissed the pleas of his wife Calpurnia, who begged him to stay away from the Capitol on that same day. She was worried that her dream of Caesar's statue gushing blood would come true. He told her that her fears were "foolish" and he was "ashamed" to yield to them, especially in light of the flattering words of Decius, the conspirator whose job it was to see that Caesar go to the Capitol to meet his death.

So what does it mean to be a good listener as a leader? To whom should a leader listen? What are some practical strategies to enhance one's capacity to listen? How does one know how and when to act based on what one hears? What about listening to your own inner voice and "following your gut"? All of these questions are critical to a leaders' capacity to make good decisions and to have sound judgment.

One of the best times to practice being a good listener as a school leader is before you even become one. Leaving the ranks of a teacher to become a school leader is life changing. Not only do the day-to-day tasks of the job change, but workdays themselves also become longer, and there are certainly more of them. In addition, the level of responsibility increases exponentially. As a teacher, one is responsible for dozens of students; as a building leader, one is responsible for hundreds of students, as well as faculty and staff.

As a building leader, one also becomes accountable to many stakeholders. All of those children have parents or guardians who have a vested interest in what happens in school. Faculty and staff need to know that they are supported in their professional decision-making and their professional learning. Faculty and staff also have bargaining unions with keen interest in their working conditions, and school leaders must be cognizant of keeping their "asks" within the confines of collectively bargained agreements. And, of course, principals report directly to district leaders, who are ultimately responsible for ensuring that a child's journey through a district meets or exceeds the expectations of the community. It is exciting and meaningful work to be a school leader. There is plenty of evidence to support the notion that the quality of the school leader has a profound impact on the academic achievement of the students in the school! So what should an aspiring leader listen for before becoming one?

FAMILY FIRST

First, an aspiring leader needs to ask their family if *they* are ready, willing, and able to support them in a role that will most definitely impact family life. The workday is longer, and there are many more evening obligations. While there is a certain rhythm to the workday, work week, and school year, there are also many unexpected twists and turns that become the responsibility of the building leader to address (or at least help to address): student discipline matters, staffing shortages, disruptions that affect the building like power outages, water main breaks, and boiler malfunctions. The list goes on and on and is especially longer if one is contemplating a move to a district leadership position; the point is that all of these things are stressful, and stress has a way of coming home and impacting family life.

Getting a new leadership position can also mean having to pick up and move a family to a new community. The implications of this transition are enormous; not only are there the financial repercussions of selling and buying real estate, which could go either way in a volatile real estate market, but a partner or spouse may need to quit a job and look for a new one. Children may need to say goodbye to familiar friends, teachers, and routines to enter the unknown. Depending on their employment skills and the job market in a new location, such a move can be an enormous sacrifice for a partner/spouse. And depending on the age of children and the extent to which they are comfortably enmeshed in their current school and community, a decision to uproot the family will have a lasting impact, for better or worse.

Before even submitting an application for a position that will require a move, leaders who aspire to the next step in their career must fully engage the family in a discussion of what such a move will mean and listen carefully to how they feel about it. If there is doubt that making a move is really doable and in the best interest of the family, one should not hit "send" on that application. It reflects poorly on a candidate to enter a search and then pull out when a position is offered because your family has lost the will to move. It also ultimately wastes valuable administrators' time, which could be better spent serving students.

It is also important to listen to what school-age children might have to say about having their parent in a leadership role in their school or district. While it might be "cool" for a kindergarten student to have mom or dad as their principal or superintendent, it will likely get less and less "cool" as that child gets older. No matter how hard a school leader may try to separate their role as principal or superintendent from being a parent, in the eyes of the staff the leader is never seen as "just" a parent. This reality has the potential to work to the benefit or the detriment of the child; maybe they are given special treatment because everyone knows who the parent is, or maybe they are held to a higher standard of achievement or behavior because of who the parent is.

What is certain, though, is that there will be awkward moments for all parties when something goes wrong: a bad decision on the part of the child or one of their good friends that requires discipline, a tough decision on the part of a coach to cut (or not) the child of a school leader from a team, or an unpopular decision on the part of the leader that angers or disappoints faculty and staff. The student is likely to hear and feel the impact of that experience. Parents who are school and district leaders need to listen carefully to what their kids say about their school experience. In the end, the whole family needs to understand what leadership entails and the leader needs to really listen to what each family member has to say about it. Everyone's happiness and the school leaders' success depend on it. Julius Caesar didn't listen to his wife's warning; it cost him his life, and, at least in the play, she was never heard from again!

READING THE ROOM

Before making any kind of career move, the wise candidate does a lot of homework to learn about the position *before* applying. Leadership preparation programs will encourage prospective candidates to research the school or district by conducting a "scan" that digs into the available data about the school or district. That data can include demographic information about the students served, their academic achievement, attendance, discipline, and participation in extracurricular activities. At the district level, that data might include information about the financial condition of the district, the integrity of the physical plant, the status of bargaining agreements, or recent media coverage of the district, all of which can signal what the imminent challenges of the job might be. This work is necessary but not sufficient for an aspiring candidate to know whether the school or district is the right place for them.

Getting a better handle on what the school and/or district are really like requires some skillful listening to those who have good insight into the organization and who have the interests of the aspiring candidate in mind. These are people with knowledge; these are people who one can trust. They are not like Decius, who knew exactly what was happening at the Capitol on March 15, 44 BC, and encouraged Caesar to go there to meet his untimely death!

So, who to trust? This is not an easy question to answer without asking a lot more questions. Who do you know with a track record of being honest, upfront, and transparent with information? Who do you know who has a reputation for making decisions that are in the best interests of the students they serve even when they are unpopular? Who do you know who has a reputation that is beyond reproach? These are the people whose advice one seeks to help them decide whether applying for a particular leadership position is a good idea.

If one doesn't know someone like this who has insight into the particular job, a candidate should still get as much insight into the position as possible from reputable sources, albeit tempering any advice with more questions: Does this person have a vested interest in the outcome of the search? Would it work to his or her advantage for the aspiring candidate to get the job, or not? Maybe they would like to see the candidate move on from their current position for their own gain. Maybe they would like to replace the candidate on their own leadership team? Julius Caesar made inaccurate assumptions about who he could trust, and it cost him dearly.

So what kind of questions should the aspiring leader ask before applying to a new position? Here are some ideas: Why did the previous leader leave? What are the people to whom one will report like? What are their values? What is their leadership style? What is their reputation? A thorough internet search might provide some insight into these questions. If you are looking to become a school principal, who is the district leader to whom you will be reporting? How long have they been in that position? What are they like to work for? Do you know anyone who works for this person well enough that you can ask that question?

If you are applying for a superintendency, who are the individual members of the board of education? What do they do (or, if they are retired, did they do) for a living? Do they have school-age children? What is the board like as a body? What do board meetings look like? Sound like? What do vote tallies tell you about their operations? Are votes split? Unanimous? A mix? Is there a lot of public commentary at the meetings? Is it handled respectfully? Is it chaotic? All of these questions can likely be answered with relatively accessible information on a district's website. What might be harder to discern is what these individuals value. What are their priorities? The best way to begin to understand that is by carefully reading the room during the interview process.

The interview (or interviews in a multi-stage search) is a critical time to tune in to the spoken and unspoken messages that the committee is sending. Pay attention to who is in the room. Is it representative of many different stakeholder groups? Who is actually asking the questions? Does every member get a chance, or does one person take on the role of lead questioner? The answers to these questions can provide insight into whether the organization believes in participatory decision-making or is more "top down" in its approach. One or the other approach might be a better fit for you. Listen carefully to the questions that the committee asks; obviously, the questions need to be answered, but the topics themselves and the emphasis placed on certain questions are windows into what is important to the school or district.

It is also important to observe the interaction of the people on the committee. Do they appear to get along? Is the room formal and stiff, or do you sense a level of comradery among the team? Are people friendly to each other? To you as the candidate? Is there any humor? After answering all of the committee's questions, are you given the chance to ask questions of them? It can be a red flag if that courtesy is not offered; it is a huge mistake for the candidate to not take full advantage of that courtesy when offered. Asking good questions of the interview committee can give excellent insight into what matters to those around the table. Good questions probe at the priorities and goals of an organization and ideally also provide some insight into how the organization hopes to achieve them. Potentially useful questions might include: What will be the top priorities for the person who gets the job? What will be the elements of an excellent first year for the successful candidate? What have been the biggest obstacles to achieving the organization's goals in the past? What support can be expected from the district as the successful candidate transitions into the new role?

Not only is it imperative to ask questions like these, but the candidate also has to listen extremely closely to the answers. What is being said? Who is saying it? What is the body language of the other committee members during the answers? It's a good sign if members are nodding enthusiastically—not a good sign if there are some who are rolling their eyes. If you are oblivious to these signs, you could be walking into a dysfunctional organization or worse. Think of our friend Julius Caesar, who was seemingly oblivious to all the signs that he was in trouble!

LISTENING ON THE JOB

If listening *before* taking the job is the difference between a good and a bad professional career decision, listening *on* the job makes even more of a difference to being successful and happy once there. Listening takes time, patience, and a commitment to honest reflection on what is heard before jumping to action. Listening also takes courage; asking the right questions sometimes reveals hard truths, and a leader has to be ready to hear it all, not just what they already know and agree with. So one must be sure to don a thick skin and try not to take hard truths personally, unless, of course, it is appropriate. (More on that subject later.)

It is fairly standard practice for leaders who are new to a building or a district to come equipped with an "entry plan." An entry plan is a document that spells out all of the activities that the new leader will engage in during the first days, weeks, months, and year in the new position. A typical element of that plan is a list of all stakeholder groups that the leader will meet with, accompanied by a collection of questions that will be asked of faculty and staff, parents, other district leaders, students, community members, and others. The questions often seek to elicit those aspects of the school or district that people are proudest of and would like to see endure; they also ask about goals and priorities that the leader should pursue. In addition, the questions might probe into those areas where stakeholders have concerns and would like to see change. Gathering this information is a critical first step in being a good listener, but it is only that—the first step.

How does a new leader make sense of all that they gather through this exercise? This is the real work. Are there themes that emerge across all groups? What are the differences across the groups? Are those differences a function of the roles played by the various stakeholder groups? There will always be competing interests that need to be balanced. For example, taxpayers will almost always say that their taxes are too high and that leaders need to control spending. Faculty and staff will almost always say that more staff is needed and that everyone needs to be paid more!

A good listener attends to all points of view, and while all points of view can be "true" from a given perspective, they cannot all empirically be in the best interest of an organization. A leader also needs to gather other data (comparative tax rates and salary schedules in this example) to inform decisions when it's time to make them. It is rare indeed for a leader to be able to make a decision that satisfies everyone. And so it is inevitable for leaders to hear "you didn't listen" from those who are dissatisfied.

One of the reasons why listening is time consuming is because it is not a "one-and-done" activity. As a new leader, it might begin with a listening tour as defined by an entry plan, but listening has to be a part of every single day. Over time, leaders learn who can be trusted to give honest, direct insight into matters unfolding in the school or district. Leaders can also figure out who those people are who share information only to advance their own agendas.

There are time-tested strategies that leaders should use to build a solid reputation and practice as good listeners. Most of these strategies are well known and easy to describe but much harder to use effectively when the busy, frequently disrupted schedule of the leader of a school building or district becomes real. For example, there is the classic "open-door policy." Lots of leaders will say that they have one, but creating a culture in which everyone feels comfortable showing up on the leaders' doorstep to share information, provide an opinion, or ask for help is far from automatic.

It is true that leaders' administrative assistants have to provide some level of gatekeeping for visitors (so that the leader can get their work done), but over time employees, parents, and community members need to see that they are welcome to speak with the leader, that they will be treated with kindness and respect, that they will be listened to with care, and that they will walk away feeling that at the very least they were genuinely "heard" even if the leader cannot give them what they may be asking for.

Perhaps a more effective strategy is "simply" being out and about and visible to stakeholders. When members of school communities are asked about the characteristics they most value and appreciate about their leaders, visibility is often at the top of the list. Being visible shows that leaders care about their school community; visibility increases access to leaders for casual exchanges that can build connections and trust and break down the barriers that teachers, students, and parents might feel if they need to go to an office with or without an appointment to be seen and heard by the leader.

All of this is common sense, but it is truly difficult to accomplish. School and district leaders have a great deal of work to do, work that is often governed by inflexible deadlines or work that arises because of an incident or crisis. Leaders are judged by how well they handle the unexpected as well as the efficiency and effectiveness of managing the day to day. Often it is not possible to get everything done, on time, and still be out and about on a regular basis. One way to improve the likelihood of doing so is to actually schedule time into the day or week when the whole point is traveling through a building or buildings to see and be seen and to listen to and actually hear people.

Other essential strategies also include answering emails in a timely fashion (or at least being upfront with individuals if there will be a delay); returning phone calls within a designated time frame, such as twenty-four hours; and always agreeing to meet with individuals who want face time. Look at every interaction as the opportunity to build a connection, forge an alliance, demonstrate genuine concern, and make sure that speakers know that they are heard. When Caesar was walking along with Antony, he made it a point that whatever Antony was saying did not literally fall on his deaf ear. Members of the school community must also be able to tell that their comments, thoughts, and suggestions are not falling on metaphorical deaf ears.

Finally, there are a number of tools that leaders can use to gather input from their communities, including surveys, focus groups, and town hall meetings. There are even online platforms that enable communities to share their thoughts and have those thoughts validated (or not) using a collective rating system that makes it possible to see which thoughts actually represent the actual majority, rather than a sometimes vocal minority. All of these tools are worthwhile and should be a part of the leaders' repertoire of listening strategies, but all of them are useless if leaders are unwilling to listen carefully and respond appropriately, even when it might be painful to do so.

THE POWER OF SPEECH

Words matter. These two words may be the most critical lesson from the play for all leaders. Think about the number of events in the play that turned because of the words spoken by key characters. Cassius, the lead conspirator, plants the seed of Caesar's tyranny in Brutus' mind by telling him stories of Caesar's past; those seeds germinate when Brutus hears that Caesar was feigning humility with the commoners who

wished him to be crowned. Cassius then gives nourishment to the growing seed of Brutus' doubts by having fabricated letters sent to Brutus'
home. The letters, written with different penmanship to suggest that the
negative opinions were widespread, were filled with more examples of
Caesar's tyrannical tendencies. These unrelenting messages ultimately
convince Brutus to turn against his friend.

Another example of the power of words is Decius' ploy to convince
Caesar to go to the Capitol on the day (the ides of March) when he was
warned by several to stay away. Decius' words were laced with flattery
and mockery and were ultimately more persuasive than the soothsayer's
warning and Calpurnia's pleading. Caesar went to the Capitol and to
his death.

Perhaps the best example of the power of words is Mark Antony's
carefully crafted "lend me your ears" speech in Act III. This skillfully
structured eulogy for Caesar ignited the people's emotions, sparked
their fury over Caesar's murder, and ultimately incited the people of
Rome to rise up against the conspirators and begin a brutal civil war.
Antony accomplished this feat even as his words insisted that Brutus
and others were "honorable men"! Finally, at the end of the play, Cassius and Brutus take their own lives when they believe they cannot win
the war, but their failure is one of communication, not military tactics.
Cassius and Brutus fail to coordinate their military strategy effectively
and spend their time arguing over who is the best soldier. Cassius
wrongly believes that his army is surrounded and ultimately takes his
own life to avoid humiliation.

The outcomes that result from miscommunication and/or the manipu-
lation of words for ambition or political gain in *Julius Caesar* are
Shakespeare's cautionary tales for all. What can school and district
leaders learn from this? There are many lessons of what to do and what
not to do with speech if one aspires to be an honorable, effective, and
successful school or district leader.

PLANTING SEEDS

Cassius used the strategy of planting seeds in order to effect change—
a destructive, conspiratorial change that was fueled by jealousy and
politically motivated. But as effective school and district leaders
know, the strategy of planting seeds can and should be used to effect

positive change in schools. Anyone who has ever been associated with schools knows that making changes, even changes for the better, can be met with significant resistance and take a very long time. Skilled leaders start the change process early by planting the seeds of ideas with stakeholders to give them time to think about what those changes might be. Perhaps a building principal would like to implement a new professional development initiative. Before rolling out a big idea, it is helpful to begin by providing bits of information, perhaps about student achievement in a particular content area, so that stakeholders begin to recognize and understand the need to take on new learning.

A superintendent might recognize the need to address some concerns with the physical integrity of district facilities. Before simply announcing the need for an expensive capital improvement project, the wise superintendent will begin to provide the school board and community with bits of information about enrollment trends, costs of repairs, and unmet needs for space as the starting point to get them thinking about the possibility of a major project. Ultimately, these "seeds" can grow into full-blown initiatives and projects that are not simply the leader's idea but the shared idea of many stakeholders who understand and embrace the reason behind the plan.

Think about how far Brutus's thinking evolved regarding Caesar. He was Brutus' trusted and revered friend, but Cassius' seeds of doubt blossomed into a full conviction that Caesar needed to be killed in order to save Rome and its republican system. Just imagine how powerful it could be to have an entire faculty fully embrace the idea of transforming instructional practices in order to improve student achievement. It can start with a small, well-placed, well-tended seed—not of doubt but of inspiration.

BIG IMPORTANT PUBLIC SPEECHES

On the other end of the continuum from seed planting, speeches are the big, important public talks that school and district leaders regularly have to deliver. Whether the event is a graduation ceremony, a budget presentation, a town hall meeting, or the opening day of school, leaders are called on to make speeches to commemorate events, to convey important information, or to inspire action.

These opportunities are critically important and absolutely must be done well. Mark Antony's famous "lend me your ears" speech is a fascinating example of how effective public speaking can be used to stir emotion, inspire loyalty, and ignite the will to act. While it is doubtful that a school or district leader will ever be charged, as Mark Antony was, with convincing an audience to seek revenge against conspirators who murdered their former leader (without appearing to do so), school and district leaders might learn a few things from how Shakespeare uses speech when planning their own. Before enumerating several cautionary lessons, a brief recap of the speech is in order.

Mark Antony is Caesar's closest and most loyal friend, and it is for that reason he is called on to speak at Caesar's funeral. Mark Antony is also savvy enough to know that the lead conspirators, particularly Cassius, do not trust him. Thus, he must be extremely careful about what he says to achieve his twofold purpose: to honor Caesar without seeming to do so and to ignite the passions of the people of Rome to rise up against the conspirators for the wrongful murder of their leader, without putting himself in harm's way with Cassius and the other conspirators.

Mark Antony begins by showing a connection to his audience. He says, "Friends, Romans, countrymen" to show that he is one of them. Throughout his speech, he shows that he is not noble like Brutus and others but a humble friend to Caesar, just as he is a "friend" to all who are gathered there to listen to him. Mark Antony is also self-deprecating about his own capacity to deliver a noble speech, saying, "I am no orator" (like Brutus), and that he is "a plain blunt man" with "neither wit, nor words, nor worth . . . nor power of speech." And then he says to the people that he is only telling them what they already know to be true. This seeming humility and personal connection to the audience win the crowd over to him.

Mark Antony then weaves references to many of Caesar's accomplishments into his remarks (conquests of other lands, filling the coffers of the city) and notes elements of Caesar's own seeming humility (weeping with the poor, turning down the offer of a crown) to suggest he was not as ambitious as Brutus and the other conspirators wanted all to believe. It was, after all, Caesar's ambition and proclivity for tyranny that were their motives for his murder. But Mark Antony is careful not to directly criticize the actions of the conspirators. In fact, he goes out of his way to praise them; nine times in the speech he calls Brutus and his colleagues "honorable men" and reminds the crowd that Brutus was Caesar's "angel" or dearest friend.

The "angel" comment is made in the midst of a long section of his speech when Mark Antony is enumerating the many stab wounds of the conspirators, the worst wound being the one that Brutus inflicted. Thus does Mark Antony thread the needle of faulting and praising Caesar and honoring and vilifying those who killed him.

Another effective ploy that Mark Antony uses is to hint that he knows the contents of Caesar's last will and testament. He suggests that it will be too sad for those listening to his speech to hear what Caesar decided to bequeath to his people. Of course, this statement piques the interest of the crowd. Mark Antony delays revealing what the will contained until the crowd is nearly overwhelmed with curiosity. At one point, he asks the crowd to gather around the body of Caesar to hear the will but then spends the next several minutes of his speech talking about the wounds that destroyed Caesar's "mantle" (or cloak) and that ultimately killed him.

Finally, after even more delay, he announces that Caesar's last will and testament bequeathed seventy-five drachmas to every Roman citizen, plus all of his private walks and orchards and gardens for their recreation and pleasure. On hearing about these many gifts to the common people, the crowd is overcome with anger and the desire to kill those who took away their kind, courageous, and generous leader.

Mark Antony's rhetoric is so effective that at one point a listener says, "We'll hear him, we'll follow him, we'll die with him." Ultimately, leaders want those they lead to be similarly (if not quite as dramatically) committed to following them. In the play, this speech is ultimately one in which Mark Antony is using rhetoric to win over the people to seek revenge for Caesar's murder. The speech energizes the people to engage in a bloody civil war through which the conspirators are brought to rough justice. It also incites chaos and mayhem; right after the speech, some citizens brutally kill an innocent man who had the misfortune of having the same name as one of the conspirators. The power of speech should not be underestimated; it can be used for good or evil, with beneficial or disastrous results. It is why leaders must use the power of speech wisely and with care.

School and district leaders are often called on to make remarks. Here are some helpful, time-tested lessons for successful public speaking.

Know Your Audience

This is the first and most important rule of effective public speaking. It is impossible to connect with an audience if one does not know who is in it. Mark Antony knew precisely who was going to be listening to him on the morning when he gave his speech to bury Caesar and thus shaped his words to connect with his friends and countrymen without offending the conspirators; both groups were listening to his words. It is not enough to simply know the category of people in one's audience; it is also important to know something about what they value and what perspectives they bring to bear on whatever the topic might be.

It is important to note that audiences are rarely monolithic in terms of the types of people in attendance and what they believe, so speakers need to find ways to connect with all. For example, in a talk about a school district's budget, the audience will be composed of many stakeholders: board members, faculty, staff, parents, students, community members without children, and business owners. All of these groups are likely to have very different needs and interests. Parents and students often want districts to spend more money on programs and services to support their children's needs. Faculty and staff are also likely in favor of more spending for programs and services, but they might emphasize increases in pay and benefits. Community members and business owners might be very supportive of the school district but might be even more mindful of increasing taxes, especially if those community members do not have children or grandchildren in the district, are on a fixed income, or are simply struggling to make a good profit with their business.

During a graduation speech, the audience will also be a mix. The primary audience is always the graduates, and the main goal is to have a message that resonates with them. But the parents, grandparents, relatives, and friends who are there supporting the graduates are also eager for a meaningful message.

Have a Clear Purpose

When giving a talk, school leaders need to be clear about their purpose. Is the purpose to share information? To honor an individual? To voice an opinion? To persuade others to take action? A budget presentation is an opportunity to share information about what is included (or not) in a particular spending plan. It should not be an opportunity to try to persuade the community to vote yes on the budget; doing so is actually expressly prohibited in states where communities vote on the school district budget. However, a speech designed to get an elected official to endorse a particular piece of legislation should certainly be informative, but it should also include a clear request for a specific action. In planning a speech, a leader needs to begin with the purpose in mind.

Mark Antony knew his audience and his purpose. He wanted the outcome to be the incitement of a rebellion against the conspirators. As soon as he finished, he said about his talk, "Now let it work. Mischief, thou art afoot,/Take thou what course thou will." When a school or district leader ends a talk, their goals (ideally not mischief) should also be afoot whether those goals are to send off a graduating class; communicate a coherent, responsible spending plan; or launch an initiative to improve the learning outcomes for students.

Have a Message

The need to have a clear message is closely related to the idea of knowing the purpose of the speech, but they are not identical. The purpose of a speech may be to share information, but what exactly are the listeners to learn? Why is it important? The purpose of a speech at graduation will likely be to celebrate the graduates, but what message should they take away? What message will resonate with them? What will they remember? What will their families take away from your comments? The answer to these questions will be "nothing" if all the speaker does is string together some platitudes.

One way to make sure a message sticks with the audience is to think about telling a brief but compelling story. People remember stories. The story can be about a personal experience or an experience shared with one or more of the members of the audience. The trick is to pick a story that gets to the heart of your message and to tell it in as few words as possible so that you engage the audience, make your point, and leave the audience wanting more, not patiently waiting for it to end. One of the stories that Mark Antony chose to tell when speaking of Caesar was how Caesar rejected the crown three times in front of the crowd at the races. His audience would certainly remember that incident, and it would absolutely refute the assertion that Caesar was ambitious, for why would he do that?

Don't Go On Too Long

"Brevity is the soul of wit." So says Polonius in Shakespeare's *Hamlet*. Sadly, Polonius is accidentally stabbed to death by Hamlet shortly after uttering these words, but they are still worth heeding when making a speech. When doing so, wise leaders know their purpose, have a clear message, and make their point without belaboring it. Sometimes it is necessary to take a lot of time to explain a complex and or detailed topic to an audience (like a board of education) that needs all of the information to make an informed decision. But during awards or commencement ceremonies, when there are often multiple speakers, it is useful to remember the advice to be brief and try to avoid anything over five minutes in length.

Mark Antony probably spoke for more than five minutes in his famous oration, but he was the only person speaking on behalf of Caesar. He also used images and stories and suspense to keep his audience interested for a long time. They begged to hear more from him and quieted their peers when he was poised to say more. The audience was *that* interested in what Mark Antony had to say. The same kind of response is a lofty goal for school and district leaders when they are before their communities.

Choose Your Words Carefully

School and district leaders should plan and write their comments well in advance of the occasion. Given the audience, the purpose, and the message, capture the words on the written page (or screen) and have those words at the podium with you. It is also wise to have a trusted colleague or mentor read your speech ahead of time to make sure it strikes the right tone and is free from words or references that could go over poorly with the audience. Unless the school leader is extremely comfortable with public speaking and particularly adept at speaking extemporaneously, it is always best to avoid saying the wrong things or somehow misspeaking by having it written down, reviewed, and practiced. While Mark Antony did not likely have a script in front of him, it is clear that he knew what he wanted to say and how he wanted to say it, with a deliberate selection of words and phrases that he knew would have the desired effect on all factions of his audience. Preparation is essential.

A lot of practicing and aspiring leaders in any field likely spend a good amount of time thinking about, and maybe even worrying about, their capacity to speak in public. Public speaking can be stressful and, for some, downright terrifying. The National Institute of Mental Health reports that public speaking anxiety, or glossophobia, affects 40 percent of the population, and some say that the fear of public speaking is even worse than the fear of death![1] Given this fact, the wise leader (aspiring or seasoned) takes the time to prepare whenever there is an opportunity to speak to their community and is thoughtful about their audience, purpose, message, and choice of words.

Shakespeare's *Julius Caesar* is a timeless play about politics and power. Like all of Shakespeare's tragedies, it is a cautionary tale, filled with lessons about what to do and what not to do. Ironically, it is the shortest play considered in this book, but it has the most to say about leadership. The essential leadership lessons in this play are about the power of words and the wisdom of being an astute listener and not just to those messages that are affirming and agreeable. The mighty Julius Caesar fell from power because he failed to pay attention to the messages that were contrary to his viewpoint and too much attention to those that simply stroked his ego. It cost him everything. School and district leaders who do not wish to follow in Caesar's footsteps, if only metaphorically, will do well to commit to listening to all with humility and intent and to speaking with purpose and integrity.

To summarize, here are some important leadership lessons from *Julius Caesar*:

1. Effective leaders are excellent listeners. They make it a point to actually hear what all stakeholders are saying to them, including those who they do not agree with and those who might be perceived to lack power or station. After listening carefully, they make decisions that are in the best interest of those they serve: students. This is not always popular.
2. Quality leaders are effective speakers. They know their audience, have a clear message, choose their words carefully, and make their

points efficiently. No rambling! These rules apply to writing as well.
3. Leaders must be able to keep confidences. Leaders learn all kinds of things about students, employees, and even community members that are meant to be kept confidential: information about health matters, disabilities, legal matters, job performance, and much more. A leader should share these things only with other individuals who absolutely need to know. Never say words to the effect of "Please don't tell anyone about this, but . . ." Few can honor that request.
4. Leaders must have humility. Even though leaders may be vested with a certain amount of power and authority, what they really have is responsibility for a lot of lives. Students, staff, and families depend on leaders to make good decisions that will keep them as safe as possible at school and ensure that they have all that they need to learn and grow in their school environment. This is a daunting task: leaders must balance the need to inspire confidence without arrogance.

DISCUSSION QUESTIONS

1. Think about a time when you failed to listen closely to someone who was offering you good advice. Why did you choose to ignore the advice? What was the outcome of your decision? What might you do differently going forward?
2. You have likely heard many graduation speeches over the course of your life. Which ones stood out to you, and why?
3. Gather some sample speeches (either your own or those of colleagues) and read them with a critical eye. Do they have a clear purpose and message? Are they tailored to the audience and of an appropriate length? Do they achieve their intended purpose? What changes might you make to them so that they are more effective and memorable?

   The final Shakespeare play to be examined is *Hamlet*, yet another tragedy that provides further insight into the leadership qualities of honesty and integrity. This play also touches on the two essential elements of effective leadership: having a clear sense of purpose and the courage to act in ways that make that purpose real.

NOTE

1. (Brewer 2001).

BIBLIOGRAPHY

Brewer, Geoffrey. 2001. "Public Speaking Anxiety." National Social Anxiety Center. March 19. Accessed July 4, 2023. https://nationalsocialanxietycenter .com/social-anxiety/public-speaking-anxiety/.

Chapter 5

Hamlet

This above all: to thine own self be true,
And it must follow, as the night the day,
Thou canst not be false to any man.

—Polonius, Act I, Scene 3

Shakespeare's *Hamlet* is among the world's great literary masterpieces. Although Shakespeare did not invent his title character or the essence of the plot, he transformed this Danish legend about a son who must avenge his father's murder into a theatrical tour de force, laced with magnificent soliloquies and stunning reversals of fortune for almost all of the main characters. It is arguably the tragedy of all tragedies, worth reading or attending again and again, an experience that should only begin in a high school English class. But beyond the high school classroom, adults can glean a great deal from this compelling and nuanced story that explores the existential questions of being, purpose, and decision-making. This learning is especially relevant to those who lead or aspire to lead schools and school districts.

Perhaps one of the reasons why this particular play is so relevant to school and district leaders is because Hamlet, like the vast majority of those who choose to work in schools on behalf of children, is fundamentally a good person. He does not have any of those ugly character flaws that make his inevitable and untimely death one that makes readers say, "Well, he got what he deserved." Hamlet is not overly ambitious like Macbeth, overly prideful like Caesar, or overly greedy, self-indulgent, or jealous like other lead characters in Shakespearean tragedies. Hamlet is a good and faithful son who loves his country, his father, his mother, his friends, and his girlfriend, Ophelia. However, he is thrust into a terrible set of circumstances by the evil of others—namely, his uncle—and he must make and try to act on very difficult decisions that can and do change the trajectory of his own life and those around him. School and district leaders are also good people, who care deeply about those they are called on to serve. Their decisions and actions can and do make profound differences in the lives of children.

SUMMARY OF *HAMLET*

Hamlet's story begins on a cold and damp night in Denmark. Officers who are on lookout duty for the kingdom witness what they believe to be the ghost of the recently deceased king, Hamlet's father. They ask Hamlet's best friend Horatio to bring Hamlet to the ramparts to verify this sighting, and he vows to do so. The next night, Hamlet joins Horatio and the others on the platform overlooking the kingdom, and sure enough, the ghost of his father appears and speaks privately to Hamlet, begging him to avenge his murder. The ghost describes in detail how his own brother, Claudius, killed him in his sleep by pouring poison in his ear and, in so doing, robbed him of "his life, his crown and his queen." This meeting with his father's ghost confirms Hamlet's darkest suspicions about his uncle, who had quickly claimed the crown of Denmark after Hamlet's father died and then, adding insult to injury, married Hamlet's mother Gertrude.

The ghost leaves no doubt that he expects Hamlet to bring his uncle to justice by killing him but to spare his mother and "leave her fate to heaven." After promising his father's ghost that he will do what is asked of him, he returns to his friends on the ramparts and asks them to keep what happened that night a secret. Thus begins Hamlet's tortured battle with himself over the if, when, and how of keeping the promise he made to his dead father.

Meanwhile, Hamlet's mother and uncle have noticed how distraught and distracted Hamlet is behaving. He is still wearing black clothing long after it would have been customary to show respect for the dead, and he seems uninterested in normal activities like returning to college or spending time with Ophelia. While Queen Gertrude is worried, his uncle is uneasy about Hamlet's behavior. Even before his encounter with his father's ghost, Hamlet was disgusted by his mother's too hasty marriage to his uncle, a man who was "no more like my father" than Hamlet was like Hercules. He says of his mother, "Frailty, thy name is woman" and "O, most wicked speed, to post/With such dexterity to incestuous sheets." He is sickened by the thoughts of his mother and uncle together, and his uncle senses something more than grief is amiss with his nephew.

Hamlet's disgust with his mother and uncle affects how he thinks of Ophelia, a lovely, obedient, and chaste young lady whom everyone assumes he will someday marry. Ophelia describes an unsettling encounter that she has had with Hamlet to her father, Polonius, who is the lord chamberlain to the king. She tells him that Hamlet came to see her in her chamber with his clothes all disheveled, took her by her wrists, and looked at her with great intensity. Then he sighed deeply and left her.

Polonius immediately wishes to tell the king what Ophelia said because it will reinforce his theory that Hamlet's unusual behavior is related to his unrequited love for his daughter. In order to curry favor with the king, Polonius offers to stage a meeting between the two young people and to eavesdrop on their exchange. It is his hope that he will hear the words that confirm the cause of Hamlet's discontent. But what everyone hears is perhaps the most famous soliloquy in all of Shakespeare, which begins, "To be or not to be, that is the question." Hamlet is indeed anguished, but over something far more grave than love: his very existence.

In the meantime, Claudius is feeling increasingly wary of Hamlet and sends for two of his childhood friends, Rosencrantz and Guildenstern, to come to the castle to try to find out what is troubling him. Their arrival coincides with that of a theater troupe, a development that seems to brighten Hamlet's mood and gives him an idea that might spur him to act on his promise. Hamlet's idea is to ask the players to insert a scene into their performance that reenacts the murder of his father by Claudius. While the scene is unfolding, Hamlet and his trusted friend Horatio will watch Claudius' face and be able to tell whether in fact he is guilty of murdering his father.

The evening of the play arrives, and the players do exactly as Hamlet has suggested. During the scene in which poison is poured into the ear of the sleeping king, Claudius becomes agitated, jumps from his seat, and demands that the play be stopped. This reaction gives Hamlet the confirmation he was craving, but circumstances prevent him from taking action. Right after the play, he sees Claudius praying in the castle chapel, where it would be a simple thing to take his life, but Hamlet hesitates. He doesn't want to kill Claudius at a time when his prayers might save his soul and make it possible for him to go to heaven rather than burn in hell as Hamlet believes he should.

Instead, Hamlet goes to see his mother in her room. He is unaware that Polonius has gone to her room ahead of him to eavesdrop on their conversation. Polonius is a foolish man who throughout the play espouses a long list of rules and maxims to his two children and others but is never taken seriously. It is Polonius who utters the famous adage from Act I, "This above all: to thine own self be true" to his son, Laertes, as the young man is about to depart for college. But the statement comes at the end of a long and rambling diatribe about what Laertes should and should not do while away from home. It is also Polonius who posits that "brevity is the sole of wit" in a conversation with the queen, but then he rambles on about Hamlet and Ophelia in a manner that is neither witty nor brief. Despite his many rules and the wisdom of some of his words, Polonius snoops on others and meddles in their business, which leads to many untimely deaths, beginning with his own.

Polonius is hiding behind a wall hanging in Gertrude's room when Hamlet confronts his mother about her marriage to her husband's brother. They exchange harsh words, and in a show of fear, Gertrude asks Hamlet whether he will murder her. When she cries for help, Polonius cries for help from his hiding place. Thinking it is Claudius, Hamlet draws his sword without any of his previous hesitations, plunges it through the wall hanging, and kills Polonius. Disappointed that he has killed an old fool and not his evil uncle, Hamlet attempts to make his mother "see" the reality of her new life by holding up a metaphorical mirror to her face.

While she may not have had a role in the murder of her first husband and may not be aware that her current husband did the deed, she is upset by Hamlet's strong rebuke of her and by his disgust that she shares a bed with Claudius. In the midst of their argument, the ghost of Hamlet's father again appears, but only Hamlet can see and hear him, so when Hamlet seems to be conversing with thin air, his mother is fully convinced that he is insane. Nevertheless, the ghost chides Hamlet for his "almost blunted purpose" to revenge his death, an action that will be postponed again. On Claudius' orders, Hamlet will be escorted to

England by his school friends, Rosencrantz and Guildenstern, where the plan is for Hamlet to be killed.

But Hamlet is very smart. He outwits his friends during their travels so that it is they who are killed, and he returns to Denmark to complete his father's bidding. When he returns, he learns that Ophelia has taken her own life. She, too, has gone mad, in part over the death of her father (at Hamlet's hand) but more likely over the inexplicable end of her relationship with Hamlet. She cannot fathom why he would turn on her so cruelly, intimating that she is not pure and chaste and telling her to get herself to a nunnery. In her final scenes on stage, she sings nonsensical songs about flowers and herbs. She drowns in a gurgling brook, surrounded by floating garlands, oblivious to her plight as her heavy skirts fill with water and drag her to the bottom to die.

Ophelia's brother, Laertes, has also returned to Denmark on learning of his father's death. At first he believes that the king is to blame for Polonius' death, but Claudius persuades him, rightly, that it was Hamlet who killed his father and that he should kill Hamlet in a duel. The king will help the plot by poisoning the tip of Laertes' rapier and a cup of wine to be sure that the job is done. Laertes and Hamlet meet at Ophelia's grave site and end up engaging in a scuffle, arguing with profound grief about who loved her more.

Shortly thereafter, Laertes challenges Hamlet to a duel, a duel that Hamlet believes is a friendly contest despite his misgivings otherwise. All of the members of the court gather to watch the young men spar. Hamlet takes an early lead, scoring the first two hits. The king encourages Hamlet to take a sip of the poisoned wine to quench his thirst, but Hamlet declines. Instead, his mother takes the chalice and drinks from it. Claudius sees what she had done, but it is too late, and she dies. Meanwhile, Laertes and Hamlet scuffle, and the tainted rapier changes hands, so that they are both hit with the poisoned tip. Realizing that they both will die, Laertes blurts out the plot he hatched with the king and shouts, "The king, the king's to blame."

The now enraged, but dying, Hamlet plunges the poisoned rapier into his uncle and forces the rest of the tainted wine down his throat, at last fulfilling the promise he made to his father, but only after the violent deaths of nearly everyone that mattered to him. As he lies dying, Hamlet asks his dear and trusted friend Horatio to "report me and my cause aright to the unsatisfied." The play ends with Hamlet being carried off stage for a soldier's burial, a brave but tortured prince whose inability to take decisive action cost many lives, including his own.

PURPOSE-DRIVEN SCHOOL LEADERSHIP

The tragedy of *Hamlet* teaches many lessons about what it means to be purpose driven. To be clear, the purpose that motivates Hamlet, to avenge the murder of his father, is *not* one that should motivate those who lead schools. But knowing what it is that one is called on to accomplish, and why, are essential elements to being an effective school leader. It is very early in the play that Hamlet suspects that "something is rotten in the state of Denmark." As the prince, Hamlet is keenly aware of his duty to the kingdom, which is why he is particularly distraught over the suspicious death of his father, the king. When he is visited by the ghost of his father, his mission as prince is made clear: Claudius killed the king to take the throne. Claudius must be killed for his treachery. Hamlet's mother must be spared since she is innocent of the murder plot, though not innocent of unseemly behavior in her "too hasty" marriage to the man who murdered her husband. The tragedy of the play is that Hamlet took too long to take action on his mission.

The best school and district leaders are also purpose driven. Their mission may not be revealed to them by a ghost, but their stakeholders in the community and their own moral compasses should guide their path forward on behalf of the children. There are many noble purposes to pursue in schools: ensuring safe and welcoming learning environments; closing achievement gaps among students and subgroups of students; ensuring that each and every student has an equitable opportunity to access rigorous programs and needed services; inspiring and supporting innovative instructional practices to prepare students for success in the world beyond school; and more. For students, going to school should be a transformational experience, but, for far too many, the experience of school is a less than inspiring exercise. At their worst, schools are complicit in replicating existing social structures that keep the wealthy and powerful in their places of privilege and everyone else at bay. There is something rotten in the system for too many children, and it is up to school leaders to do something about it, but, like Hamlet, they often struggle to take the action to make it better, mostly because doing so is really hard.

To illustrate just how difficult it is to take action on a purpose that a leader knows to be the right thing to do, consider the challenge of moving a school or district to be more equitable and inclusive for each and every student, regardless of their race, religion, economic status, gender, gender identity, sexual orientation, or dis/ability status. Equity work is purportedly high on many leaders' list of priorities, but actually making it happen is more of a rarity. There are plenty of data to illustrate how certain categories of students are treated poorly, left behind, or just plain forgotten in many schools across the nation.

For example, students with disabilities are often not fully included in the classrooms of their school communities. When students are struggling academically or behaviorally, there is too often a tendency to want to remove those students from their classrooms. They are suspended from school for disciplinary reasons at a disproportionate rate, placed in segregated settings away from their non-disabled peers, held in restraints, and detained in padded rooms; they can even be the victims of corporal punishment. Removing children from their classrooms denies them access to the curriculum, quality instruction, and the positive role models of their non-disabled peers, so the children who struggle the most in school end up facing even more barriers to learning than their actual disability. Ironically, the very purpose of special education services is to remove barriers to learning!

Everyone knows that such treatment is wrong, but it still happens in some school settings. There are many reasons why this treatment continues. Among them is the valid concern that faculty and staff don't have the resources and support they need to help students with disabilities succeed in a general education classroom. Despite a decades-old federal mandate that students with disabilities be educated in "the least restrictive environment," the federal government has never even come close to providing the funding to schools to make that mandate truly doable. Local resources fund the vast majority of programs and services to support students with disabilities. Those costs are enormous, sometimes even financially crippling for districts, but still not sufficient to meet the needs of some students.

There are also concerns from the families of other children who do not want their school experience disrupted by another student who is struggling. Although there is plenty of research to support the notion that students with disabilities benefit from being with their non-disabled peers, and vice versa, creating an environment where that is the case is difficult. It involves a transformation of the hearts and minds of all stakeholders in a school community to accept the differences of others and to understand that their own children will not be somehow short-changed academically if they are learning with other students with a range of abilities.

Without a doubt, teaching a classroom of children with wide-ranging ability levels requires a commitment to do so, considerable expertise, and appropriate supports like co-teachers, paraprofessionals, planning time, and professional development. Because all of these efforts are difficult and costly, there are too many instances in which students with disabilities are sent "somewhere else"—a special classroom down the hall, a special program in another school, or a special placement in another community.

A similar story can be told about the experiences of students of color. Black and brown students are disproportionately suspended from school for misbehavior, tend to lag behind their peers in achievement on standardized tests, are less likely to be enrolled in higher-level courses like advanced placement, and are disproportionately referred to com-mittees on special education for classification. Students of color are also on the receiving end of everything from macroaggressions ("You are so articulate!" or "Can I touch your hair?") to overtly racist remarks like being called the "n" word. Even worse, too many children of color do not even bother to report their negative experiences to their teachers or school and district leaders because they do not believe it will make a difference. Too often, it is their perception that "nothing will be done."

People of color are often blatantly excluded from the curriculum. The accomplishments of great leaders, inventors, scientists, writers, artists, and musicians of color are glossed over or completely ignored except for during a special month each year. Many African American students experience an American history that has been "white-washed." The devastating and demoralizing story of the slave trade and the use of slaves in creating the wealth and power of the United States is never fully told. And too often when an attempt is made to broach the topic of slavery in a classroom, all eyes turn awkwardly to the black stu-dents in class, as if by their very color they can or should shed light on America's history. And lately this subject, like the next one, is need-lessly politicized.

Another group of students who often feel less than welcomed and affirmed in schools are students in the lesbian, gay, bisexual, transgender, and/or queer (LGBTQ+) community. LGBTQ+ students are among those who experience the most anxiety about being in school. They are often fearful of being found out, unsure of who they can trust, and self-conscious about their appearance. As a result, they often experience isolation and loneliness. Data gathered on the school experience of LGBTQ+ students show that their attendance is poor, they are among the most likely to be bullied by their peers, and they are at great risk for engaging in self-harm, including suicide. It is no wonder that they do not want to come to school.

Many other marginalized groups feel less than welcomed and affirmed in our nation's schools. Students who practice different religions, students who are learning English as a new language, students who are poor, homeless students, students who have a physical disability, and students who are overweight all have a tough time fitting in and feeling like they belong at school. Like Hamlet knowing that what Claudius did was wrong, school and district leaders worth their salt know that it is wrong for any student to feel excluded from the very institutions whose mission is to serve them. But making real, measurable change for those very students is elusive.

And it is not for lack of effort. For example, educational leaders, like Hamlet, spend a lot of time verifying the problems they observe in schools. Hamlet sensed something was wrong with how his uncle became king. His hunch was confirmed by the arrival of none other than the ghost of his dead father. Yet Hamlet still wanted more confirming information, so he worked with the traveling theater troupe to stage an elaborate reenactment of his father's murder, so he could watch the reaction of the guilty party. Hamlet's plan worked perfectly. He had his confirmation of Claudius's guilt. There should have been nothing stopping him from taking the action he had promised his father, an action that would have made him, as prince, the rightful heir to the throne. But Hamlet found a reason not to act when he had the chance. He certainly didn't want to send a murderer directly to heaven—or so he feared.

School and district leaders look at all kinds of data and information to verify any number of problems in schools, including the ones noted above. They read the educational research, conduct their own surveys, gather their own quantitative data, and convene focus groups to gather qualitative data. When it comes to issues of diversity, equity, and inclusion, all of that data confirms that there are too many marginalized groups of children who are not well served by our schools. They don't feel safe, welcomed, or affirmed. They are disciplined disproportionately. Their attendance is poor. They suffer from anxiety and school phobia. Their achievement lags. Why aren't leaders acting to change this situation?

The answer, to be fair, is that many educational leaders do act to take on the tough challenges facing today's schools. In recent years, interest in addressing issues of diversity, equity, and inclusion in schools has exploded. School districts are creating equity committees and task forces, hiring equity officers, conducting equity audits, writing equity plans, providing professional learning opportunities to faculty and staff, reviewing curriculum to assess and amend its inclusivity, and taking stock of library collections to make sure that they contain titles that serve as both windows and mirrors to the students of the school. All of this work is excellent, needed, and overdue. It also takes real courage to lead and support these efforts, because there are many in the United States who do not like this work and are pushing back, sometimes vigorously.

There are those who object to discussions around race because they believe that confronting this centuries-old problem will make white children feel guilty. There are those who object to creating heterogeneous classrooms that represent a wide range of ability levels because they do not want their children near "those kids" who might slow things down. There are those who do not want schools to acknowledge LGBTQ+ issues because they fear that doing so will promote sexual experimentation in their own children; they fear that their children are being "groomed" to be gay, or lesbian, or transgender. Of course, none of this is true, but that hasn't stopped those who object from taking action. Demands from parents to ban books from classrooms and school and public libraries is at an all-time high. School board elections have become hotly contested, with candidates espousing messages about "taking back their schools" all over the nation. Some states are banning a stunning array of books, everything from picture books about the pride flag to the classics like *To Kill a Mockingbird* and a graphic adaptation of *The Diary of Anne Frank*. When these kinds of responses occur, school and district leaders are in the crosshairs.

Herein lies another parallel with *Hamlet*. After the play-within-a-play scene, Claudius was certain that Hamlet knew that he had killed his father to take the crown and the queen as his wife. Claudius knew that if he were to hang on to his power, Hamlet needed to go. That was when he hatched the plan for Rosencrantz and Guildenstern to accompany

Hamlet to England carrying a letter that called for the authorities there to kill him.

When power and privilege are threatened, those who have it do their best to sideline those who threaten it. In twelfth-century Denmark, that was done with poison and duels. In current times, when those with power and privilege sense they might be losing ground, they fight back with tactics like voter suppression, misinformation campaigns, and trumped-up reasons for school leaders to lose their jobs. It is no wonder that school and district leaders tread lightly with these challenging topics. But, like Hamlet, they need to outsmart those who, under the pretense of protecting their children, are trying to stop progress in the effort to serve each and every child.

TO DO OR NOT TO DO: THAT IS THE QUESTION

Beyond a leader's understanding of and commitment to their purpose is the essential skill of decision-making. Arguably, there is no more famous exploration of existential decision-making than Hamlet's "To be or not be" soliloquy at the midpoint of the play. Hamlet is bereft, desperate, and frustrated with himself. He knows that his purpose is to avenge his father's murder by killing Claudius, but he has failed to act and now wonders whether he would be better off ending his own life. Ultimately, Hamlet decides not to take his own life because he doesn't know whether what he will encounter in the afterlife will be even worse than the misery he is feeling on earth. Hamlet does not act on his suicidal thoughts, but immediately after exploring them, he projects his misery and disgust onto the person who deserves it least in the play: the woman he used to love, Ophelia. He unceremoniously tells her to get to a nunnery and that he never loved her. Ironically, she does in fact commit suicide, though without any of Hamlet's perseveration. When she accidentally falls into the brook, she simply doesn't bother to try to save herself. Hamlet's inability to make and act on a decision had dire consequences for his one-time love.

The decisions that school and district leaders have to make also have profound effects on those they lead. To be clear, many of the decisions that have to be made in schools and districts are part of a process in which input from a variety of stakeholders is sought, reviewed, and weighed. But there are critical times when the leaders need to make the call: Who to recommend for hire? Who to recommend for tenure? How long to suspend a student for a serious violation of the code of conduct? How to respond to a threat to school safety?

The course of action that leaders take will make a difference in countless lives, and the matter of school safety can literally be a matter of life and death. Decision-making is a lonely part of the job. It is often difficult to know what course of action is the right one; leaders need to be ready to live with the consequences. They also need to understand that they will own the outcome because even if a decision is made as part of a shared decision-making process, there is no such thing as shared responsibility or accountability; that is reserved for the leader.

Hiring Decisions

Every well-run school district should have a well-defined set of procedures for recruiting and hiring new members of the school and district team. Regardless of the type of position, everything from bus driver to lunch monitor to teacher to principal to assistant superintendent, those procedures likely spell out the essential elements of the job posting. Those elements can include the types of information that will be gathered from prospective candidates and the sequence of events associated with the interview process, including who screens applicants, who participates on interview committees, the function of those committees, how job offers are made, how salaries are set, and so much more. There might also be some larger overarching goals of the organization that need to be factored into the process, such as an interest in enhancing the diversity of the district's employees to better match the backgrounds and experiences of the students served.

There are certainly times when going through the hiring process leads to a candidate who is the obvious front-runner. The candidate has all the requisite knowledge, skills, dispositions, and certifications/licenses and hits it off with everyone on the interview committee, has great references, and is an excellent fit for the school building or district position. Offering this person a position is an easy choice. But more often than not, there is not a clear choice: equally qualified candidates might have very different personalities, histories, or philosophies that cause different members of interview committees to prefer different candidates.

Sometimes there is a choice between an internal candidate and a person who would be new to the school community. Though not equally qualified on paper, some members of an interview team might advocate for an internal candidate who is a known entity, or who is well connected, rather than take a chance on someone who is not already well known. Or perhaps no single strong candidate emerges and the committee is struggling to pick from mediocre choices, a phenomenon that happens more frequently as labor shortages impact schools, especially in certain titles and content areas.

It is when there is no clear choice that school and district leaders are in the position of making the call about who to pick. It is only the district leader who can ultimately make the recommendation to the board of education about who to hire. It is a tremendous responsibility to make a recommendation about who will drive students to school, teach them to read, keep them safe and secure in the school buildings, and make decisions about the day-to-day experience of school. Ultimately, district leaders need to do what Hamlet did: gather as much information from trusted sources as possible, listen carefully to what individuals say and what others say about them, and observe closely how they interact with others. Then district leaders need to act timely and decisively to get the best candidates; perseverating too long about whether to hire could well mean that good candidates get scooped up by neighboring districts also trying to hire quality people.

Tenure Decisions

Another key decision point that lands with school and district leaders is whether to recommend teachers and administrators for a tenure appointment at the end of their probationary period. When certificated staff members are awarded tenure, they earn significant rights that protect them from discipline or dismissal even if their job performance becomes substandard. A tenure recommendation means that the district is prepared to make a professional lifetime commitment to an individual. Not only does such a recommendation have profound implications for hundreds or even thousands of students a teacher might encounter over a thirty-year career, but it is also an enormous financial commitment. When a district grants tenure to a teacher making $60,000 per year, it translates into close to a $3M investment over the next thirty years (assuming a roughly 3 percent salary increase each year). This dollar investment is for salary alone and does not include the significant costs associated with health insurance coverage and other benefits.

Chapter 5

Just like with hiring, the decision to tenure someone can be very obvious. After three to four years of service that have been thoroughly and appropriately observed and assessed, it should be clear whether the person should become a permanent member of the team. Frankly, if there are doubts along the way, a significant level of intervention and support and its impact would signal the need to discontinue the employment relationship long before the end of a probationary period.

In reality, however, there are times when the decision is not so easily made. One way that tenure decisions get muddied is when the immediate supervisor of the probationary employee, for whatever reason, does not adequately observe, evaluate, and document the performance of that employee. Sometimes this is the result of insufficient supervision; it just doesn't get done. Sometimes this happens when there is turnover in the supervisory role partway through the employee's probationary period. It may take some time for the new person to get to know the work of their staff.

Sometimes different supervisors have different opinions on what they value in an employee, so the first supervisor may think the person is outstanding, but the new person sees problems in their performance. Sometimes the record could be a mix of positive and negative, but the person is a teacher in a highly specialized content area where finding a replacement might be next to impossible, so ending the employment of the person might also spell the end of the program. When the record of performance is incomplete, or has conflicting information, it is up to the district leader to decide whether to make a recommendation to tenure an individual.

Although not quite as dramatic as Hamlet's internal debate to take his own life, the district leader is also weighing a decision that will affect the lives of many children, the life of the employee, and taxpayers, too. Like Hamlet, that leader will ponder the pros and cons of a tenure or termination determination, knowing that deciding to tenure might be the easier course of action in the short term but prove harmful over time. Deciding to terminate will likely upset many in the short term: the individual who might be surprised that there was a problem, the bargaining unit that protects the rights of its members, students and parents who might be fond of the individual, and the board of education that might be wondering how an employee could spend three or four years working in the district and to have their job performance emerge as an issue very late in the game. These are all legitimate concerns that a district leader will need to consider and address.

Ironically, while the leader is pondering the job performance of the probationary employee, others will be questioning the leader's job performance. This last-minute scramble to decide may ultimately reflect more negatively on them than the employee to be terminated. Why didn't you do your job? Why didn't you make sure that those who report to you did their job to supervise staff? These are fair questions that should inspire some organizational improvements. But is the pressure enough to make a leader tenure someone they do not have full confidence in? It shouldn't be!

Hamlet ultimately delayed taking any action when considering killing himself. He also delayed taking action on avenging the murder of his father. In tough tenure decisions, delay is also an option. With the agreement of the affected employee, their union representation, and the board of education, a leader can recommend and execute an agreement that extends the probationary period to an agreed-on amount period of time. Such an extension allows for more supervision, observation, evaluation, and documentation before a final decision about tenure is made. Ultimately a decision must be made; school and district leaders need to use the time wisely to inform that decision, or the ending could lead to instructional disaster or just non-optimal performance outcomes. The right decision, whether in hiring or granting tenure, is always the one that honors the best interests of students over the long term.

Safety Decisions

Hiring and tenure decisions are just two areas where the district leader needs to make the call, but there are others that are also very difficult and can and do have enormous impact on the lives of others. Determining the appropriate length of a student's suspension for a serious violation of the code of conduct is one. Making threats, fighting, selling drugs, or bringing weapons to school must carry serious consequences, but how long should a student be banned from coming to school? Do suspensions change behavior? Do suspensions inspire students to buckle down on their school work or mean that they will fall behind academically? District leaders need to make decisions for individual students that can and do change the trajectory of their school experience. These decisions also send a message to the entire school community about how seriously their leader takes the safety of the rest of the students and faculty in a building.

Another difficult decision point is making the call about whether to delay or close school because of inclement weather. The default position is that school should be open; there is a minimum number of days that it must be in session, for both academic and financial reasons. It is a positive thing for students to be in school, with their teachers and peers, learning. There are also dollars attached to each day a school district is open, and it is up to school leaders to make sure their district hits that mark. But when the weather is bad, or predicted to be bad, someone needs to make the call about whether it is safe to have school buses on the road. While the district leader can get lots of input from their transportation and maintenance team, as well as from weather prediction experts, ultimately they must make the call and deal with the fallout of a potentially bad decision.

EYES ARE WATCHING

To hire or not to hire, to tenure or not to tenure, to suspend or not to suspend, to close or not to close—these are the questions that keep school district leaders up at night! To make matters even more stressful, the answers to these questions are closely scrutinized and critiqued by many, and it is a rare decision that is applauded by all. School and district leaders need to be prepared to be under the microscope, just as Hamlet was.

A recurring theme throughout *Hamlet* is spying. Characters are constantly spying on one another for one reason or another. Polonius is perhaps the most notorious spy in the play. He sends spies to watch his son Laertes at school in France because he doesn't trust him to behave. He spies on Hamlet and Ophelia in order to confirm his theory that Hamlet is insane over unrequited love. Polonius also spies on Hamlet and Gertrude when Hamlet confronts his mother for her hasty marriage to Claudius. He is hiding behind a wall hanging, listening to their conversation when he is so unceremoniously killed by Hamlet.

Claudius is also into spying on Hamlet. He enlists the help of Hamlet's former schoolmates Rosencrantz and Guildenstern to keep an eye on their old friend and to report to the king about his behavior. Even Hamlet engages in his own version of spying when he enlists the players of the theater troupe to reenact the murder of his father during their performance at the castle so that Hamlet and Horatio can watch the reaction of Claudius. It is this spying that confirms Hamlet's suspicions that Claudius is guilty. There is even a bit of supernatural spying in the play, as Hamlet's father comes back from the dead to inform his son of the nature of his death, to charge Hamlet to avenge his murder by killing Claudius, and then to chide him when he procrastinates too long. While it might not be spying exactly, school and district leaders are definitely watched. Faculty, staff, students, parents, community members, other elected officials, and the media all pay close attention to the things their school leaders say and don't say, do and don't do. And it doesn't stop there. People pay attention to the cars they drive, the clothes they wear, the amount of vacation time they take, and just about any other aspect of one's personal life that can be seen. Not only do they pay attention, but they also judge. And for the most part, those judgments are made and discussed outside of the earshot of leaders: on social media, in the stands at athletic events, and at parties and other gatherings where adult stakeholder groups are together.

School leaders and superintendents should be judged on the quality of their leadership and decision-making on the job. A community has entrusted its children into the hands of school and district leaders. There is nothing more precious than a community's children, so providing a safe, welcoming learning environment where each child has the full opportunity to grow and develop physically, intellectually, and socially is the right expectation for leaders, one for which they should be held accountable.

Communities also entrust a tremendous amount of their money to school and district leaders, and they should be judged for how responsibly and effectively they use those resources to support children. That judgment is made publicly each year when school district budgets are voted on by their community. It is naïve to think that a referendum on a budget is just about dollars and cents. It is absolutely a judgment on the job performance of the person (the superintendent) and people (board of education) ultimately responsible for bringing that budget forward. This is as it should be, and leaders should be ready to handle that kind of pressure, scrutiny, and judgment.

Regardless of whether the scrutiny of other aspects of a leader's life is fair, it is simply part of the package of being a leader. This is especially true for a school or district leader, whose salary is paid with tax dollars. Driving an expensive car or appearing less than professional in demeanor or attire, even after hours, can get people talking. School and district leaders are wise to think about being "on the job" even when the school day or school year has ended. Being a school or district leader is more than a job; it is a way of life. That's why, at the end of the day, leaders truly need to know themselves, their values, their strengths, their weaknesses, their capacity to make courageous decisions, and their ability to weather both positive and negative judgment and critique. Being a school or district leader is not for the faint of heart.

Perhaps one of the most famous lines in *Hamlet* is the wise adage "To thine own self be true." At face value, this line seems to be an encouragement for all to be true to themselves and their values. It appears to be a statement encouraging honesty, integrity, and a strong moral compass. However, the line is spoken by one of the least reliable (and even a little foolish) characters in the play—Polonius. No one, and especially the title character, takes him seriously. He speaks this line at the end of a long speech to his son, Laertes, just before he is about the return to university. The gist of the speech is for Leartes to look out for himself and his own self-interests. He is told "to never a borrower or lender be," not because debt is potentially problematic but because it is not in his own personal self-interest to either help someone or need help from others.

It may never be clear what Shakespeare meant by putting such profound words into such a foolish mouth in the play, but for those who lead schools and districts, the face value of a statement about being true to yourself is in fact a priceless bit of advice. The only way to be successful and happy in the demanding world of leading schools and districts is to be true to yourself and your values.

Here is a summary of leadership lessons from *Hamlet*:

1. Effective leaders do not simply sustain the status quo of their schools and districts. They are always leading with the purpose of improving the learning environment for their students. Know and embrace the mission that drives you. Lead with purpose.
2. Any purpose worth pursuing will require leading others out of their comfort zone, and this task takes courage. Whether your purpose is ensuring safe and welcoming learning environments, closing achievement gaps among students and subgroups of students, ensuring equitable access to rigorous programs for all students, or

inspiring and supporting innovative instructional practices, it will require others to make changes to their beliefs, their perspectives, and/or their way of doing things. It is not work for the faint of heart.

3. Leaders should always engage and listen to the thoughts of stakeholders when making decisions. But there are times when a decision rests solely (or nearly so) on the leader. When faced with a difficult decision, the most effective leaders think through all of the implications, or ripple effects, of the various options in all aspects of the organization. Ultimately, they must make a decision that will be in the best interests of children over the long term.

4. Be ready to be watched. Faculty, staff, students, parents, community members, elected officials, and the media pay close attention to the things that their school and district leaders say and do. School and district leaders are often the highest-paid professionals in their community; they are also paid with tax dollars, so many believe that they have the right to observe and judge that leader. Strive to live a life that is beyond reproach.

DISCUSSION QUESTIONS

1. What purpose drives your work as a school or district leader? What is the "why" that inspires this work? What are the challenges associated with leading with that purpose? What progress have you made toward that purpose? What are the benefits for students?

2. Think about a time when you had to make a difficult decision. What were the circumstances? What process did you use to make the decisioncall? What was the outcome? If you could do it over again, would you change anything?

3. Hamlet was tormented throughout the play because he knew what had to be done to avenge his father's death, but he simply could not make himself do it until it became a crisis. As a result, his procrastination cost the lives of all of the main characters, save one (Horatio). Have you ever observed or been a part of a set of circumstances in which the appropriate action was obvious, but those in charge delayed responding until it was too late? What happened? What recommendations would you make to improve the outcome?

Conclusion

Shakespeare was not an expert in education. There are only a few passing references to school in his plays, and it is unlikely that he could ever imagine what a K–12 school in the United States in the early twenty-first century is like. So it may seem that the leap from Shakespeare's nearly five-hundred-year-old plays to educational leadership in the 2020s is enormous. But leading in schools and school districts is an intensely human endeavor; it is the complex work of coordinating and inspiring teams of people to make the magic of learning happen for a community's most precious resource: its children. To lead such an endeavor, one needs the gift of understanding how human beings think and feel, act and react, and hope and dream. And that is where Shakespeare's expertise comes in: he is masterful in bringing to life the highs and lows of the human condition.

Lessons from the Bard: What Shakespeare Can Teach Us about School District Leadership offers a window into five of Shakespeare's most well-known plays—*Romeo and Juliet, Macbeth, The Merchant of Venice, Julius Caesar,* and *Hamlet*—to allow school leaders to hold up a mirror to themselves and ask: What kind of a leader am I? Do I truly understand how children learn and develop, or do I have more to learn? Do I make sure that each and every child is seen, heard, welcomed, and affirmed, or do some feel "othered" in my school? Do I lead with a shared mission-driven purpose or simply manage the status quo? Can I show mercy? Do I have a tragic flaw?

These and so many other essential leadership questions are prompted by the words and deeds of some of the most memorable characters in all of literature. But Shakespeare wrote thirty-three other plays, not mentioned in these pages, that most certainly hold powerful insights into what it means to be an effective leader. Perhaps a look into some of them is warranted. However, the five selected for this book hold a certain level of poetic justice for educators who lead schools that likely require students to read one or more of these texts. And the truth is that students often struggle through the dense language and unfamiliar vocabulary of Elizabethan English to get to the gem of the story and its themes. School leaders can take this opportunity to reflect on the many lessons shared here. Their struggle will not be with language but might be with what they see in themselves when they hold up that mirror.

So many of the lessons that can be drawn from Shakespeare are cautionary. That is, a leader does not want to be overly ambitious like Macbeth, too easily swayed by flattery like Caesar, or too stymied by indecision to take action like Hamlet. These and many other character flaws are the hallmarks of tragedy in drama. And while school leaders certainly seek to avoid both tragedy and drama in their work, there is so much more to their work than avoiding disaster. The real goal is to serve a school community with honesty and integrity and from a place of genuine commitment to the well-being and success of each and every student. This work is more than a job; it is a calling. It is work that can be all consuming and frustrating, but it also brings precious moments of profound joy and intense satisfaction, as anyone who has ever handed a diploma to a student who struggled through high school can attest.

Perhaps the most important lesson for school leaders is spoken by Polonius in *Hamlet* when he says to his son, Laertes, who is about to return to university in France, "To thine own self be true." Coincidentally, Polonius says these words to Laertes in one of the rare references to school in all of Shakespeare. The best school leaders are individuals who know themselves well and aspire to be the best versions of themselves, not for fame or glory or wealth, but rather because they care about children, their communities, and everyone's future. In the end, that is what's at stake.

About the Author

Marie Wiles has been an educator for over thirty-five years. She began her career as a secondary school English teacher, where she relished the opportunity to share the wonders of reading and writing about great literature with her high school students. Shakespeare's *Romeo and Juliet*, *Macbeth*, *The Merchant of Venice*, and *Hamlet* were among the titles through which she invited young readers to evolve from feeling daunted to delighted by the complexity and nuance of Shakespeare's language, his compelling characters, and his keen insight into human nature.

Marie has served in several leadership roles, including curriculum development specialist, director of curriculum and instruction, and assistant superintendent for curriculum and instruction at two boards of cooperative educational services in New York. In that capacity, she led and supported the professional learning of teachers during a time when New York was adopting new standards, assessments, and accountability standards to meet federal requirements.

Marie became the district superintendent at the Otsego Northern Catskills BOCES in 2001, a dual role that involved leading the agency that served nineteen small rural school districts in upstate New York and serving as the state commissioner's representative in the field for that region. At thirty-eight, Marie was the youngest woman to be hired to serve as a BOCES district superintendent in New York State and the only one to become a mother while in that role.

Since 2010, Marie has served as the superintendent of schools for the Guilderland Central School District. In addition to her commitment to providing top-notch learning opportunities for each and every one of the five thousand students enrolled in her district, she is deeply committed to supporting the development of future school leaders. She has been a faculty member of the Superintendent Development Program through SUNY Oswego and a frequent presenter for events sponsored by the New York State Council of School Superintendents, including their statewide conferences, the Aspiring Superintendent Program, and the Women's Initiative. Marie has also served on the Executive Committee of NYSCOSS and the Governing Board of American Association of School Administrators.